HARD CASE

THE AUTOBIOGRAPHY OF
JIMMY CASE
WITH ANDREW SMART

JOHN BLAKE

Published by John Blake Publishing Ltd,
3 Bramber Court, 2 Bramber Road,
London W14 9PB, England

www.johnblakepublishing.co.uk

www.facebook.com/johnblakebooks
twitter.com/jblakebooks

This edition published in 2014

ISBN: 978 1 78219 994 6

British Library Cataloguing-in-Publication Data:

A catalogue record for this book is available from the British Library.

Design by www.envydesign.co.uk

Printed in Great Britain by CPI Group (UK) Ltd

1 3 5 7 9 10 8 6 4 2

Papers used by John Blake Publishing are natural, recyclable products made
from wood grown in sustainable forests. The manufacturing processes
conform to the environmental regulations of the country of origin.

Every attempt has been made to contact the relevant copyright-holders,
but some were unobtainable. We would be grateful if the
appropriate people could contact us.

CONTENTS

ACKNOWLEDGEMENTS

I would like to sincerely thank Andy Smart for working so tirelessly with me on this book. And a big thanks to Pete and Julie Byrne as well – without their help and support the book would never have happened.

FOREWORD

They talk a lot about role models these days, and any kid with dreams of becoming a footballer could do no better than follow the example of Jimmy Case.

He came to Liverpool from the non-league for about £10,000, which was nothing really, and I related to him straight away because I had been signed two years earlier for £33,000 – another modest fee – so we were both in the same situation; neither of us came in with a big bang.

I knew what everyone would be thinking about Jimmy because they had probably thought the same about me when I signed for Liverpool from Fourth Division Scunthorpe: 'Good luck son, but it won't be easy to get in the team here… not if you only cost £10,000.'

So expectation was zilch, but I had been in that position as well. I knew it could be done. And from day one he impressed everyone; not in an out-of-the-ordinary way but as someone who could do everything that was asked of him. He wasn't flash, he knew his place, he didn't upset the apple cart, and he just fitted in. But what would you expect? Everybody gets on well with Jimmy Case.

It was like that on the pitch just as much as off it because he was so easy to play with. The best way I can describe it is to say that Jimmy did exactly what it says on the tin. You knew what you were going to get and Jimmy knew what he could give you. He never tried to do things he knew he couldn't do, and everything he did do was eight or nine out of ten; good fitness, good ball retention, a footballing brain, an understanding of the team ethic. That's why he got in the side and stayed in it.

Well, there *was* one exception: I would give him ten out of ten for shooting. I would put Jimmy in the same class as Peter Lorimer; in terms of pace and power, they were the two outstanding kickers of a ball that I have ever had the pleasure of seeing.

I think that perhaps, because he had this reputation as a hard man, he was underrated as a footballer – but not by the Liverpool players and certainly not by the Liverpool fans, and they are the best judges.

I was with him at a match recently and you know what? The fans still love him. Jimmy is the kid who had gone to watch the games and then got signed to play the game himself. The fans see themselves in Jimmy. They see Jimmy as someone who was living his dream and they look at him and think 'that could be me'.

That's why he is so popular. Jimmy won't mind me saying this, because it is also said about me: we weren't the most talented players but we got past many others who were better than us by doing the simple things well. Not looking for the world-beating ball, but looking for the right ball, and that's what Jimmy did. I have maximum respect for him.

I suppose the one thing in his career he may look back on with disappointment is that he never played for England. Why? It's a mystery to me. There was a certain period in his career when he could have played internationals, when he should have been in squads, but the only people who can answer that question would be the England managers at the time.

My own opinion is that he suffered because there were so many Liverpool players in the squad and the England managers just didn't want to pick another one. There were six at one time in a Ron Greenwood squad, plus me as an ex-Liverpool player; I think that worked against Jimmy. It wasn't right, but it's the only reason I can give. It's not as if there were hundreds of better players around at the time, that's for sure!

But, credit to Jimmy, he just got on with it; it was something that was beyond his control and worrying about it wasn't going to help him. That was Jimmy's strength. He kept going, week after week, playing for a top club, in a team that was winning things, never letting his standards drop.

That's why I think this book will be of great interest, because it's not just about the things he did, it's also about things he should have achieved and didn't; it will open up a debate among Liverpool supporters because I know a lot of them have said that there were many worse players than Jimmy Case who won caps for England… and they would be absolutely right.

Knowing Jimmy as I do, I doubt if it keeps him awake at night. He just loved playing football and he wanted to play for as long as he could for anyone who wanted him. I finished at thirty-three, Jimmy went on until he was forty-one.

That tells you everything you need to know.

Kevin Keegan

CHAPTER ONE

WEMBLEY AND ME

I can roll back the film in my mind as if it just happened yesterday.

It is 6 May 1977, and the old Wembley Stadium is rocking. There are 99,250 people packed into the great stadium with its Twin Towers, a sea of red as fans of Manchester United and Liverpool chant and sing, with dreams of the greatest domestic prize in world football... the FA Cup.

As if there wasn't enough pressure from the crowd and the millions of TV viewers around the world, both teams were desperate to win.

United were hell-bent on lifting the cup because only the year before they had been shocked and humiliated by unfancied Southampton with that winning goal, scored by Bobby Stokes, coming out of the blue.

And we were Liverpool, cock of the North, all our focus on

securing a unique treble. Already we had won the Division One title, but not only was the elusive League and Cup double on the cards, four days later we would face Borussia Möenchengladbach in the European Cup final. History was there to be made.

We knew it wasn't going to be easy; there was never a chance of us underestimating the opposition, even though we were the champions. Our manager, Bob Paisley, and his coaches, Joe Fagan, Ronnie Moran and the rest of the boot room boys, would never let that happen. Arses would be kicked if any sign of complacency was shown, but we really fancied our chances.

And we knew what we were up against. United were definitely on the rise again with Tommy Docherty in charge, and they had some class players: Alex Stepney in goal, Martin Buchan, Jimmy and Brian Greenhoff, Stuart Pearson and Lou Macari, with Gordon Hill and Steve Coppell on the wings.

Hey, but we weren't so bad either.

This was our line-up: Ray Clemence, Phil Neal, Joey Jones, Tommy Smith, Ray Kennedy, Emlyn Hughes, Kevin Keegan, Yours Truly, Steve Heighway, David Johnson and Terry McDermott. Substitute: Ian Callaghan.

It was set up to be a great game. Two top teams. For weeks ahead of the final, the media and the supporters had been building it up to be one hell of a clash and all the ingredients were there. We started out as favourites but, as we all know, cup ties can be unpredictable and the Wembley factor just made it an extra-special test.

It was only my second season as an Anfield professional but

I don't remember any great worry or nervousness. This was what I had dreamed about as a kid playing in the streets of Liverpool: walking out at Wembley Stadium to take part in an FA Cup final and, best of all, in a Liverpool strip. They had been my team for as long ago as I could remember.

The atmosphere during the build-up was immense, all the hopes and the expectation. We were just twelve ordinary blokes and there we were, representing the red half of our wonderful city, the dreams of the faithful resting on our shoulders. And as we walked into the stadium, the fans surrounded us. I remember one shouting, 'Go 'ed, Jimmy lad, sort em out!' and that type of thing hits home. That was the sort of relationship I always had with the fans: they knew I would give them everything.

As I strolled onto the pitch with my buddy, Ray Kennedy, the sun was beating down. But then again, it always seemed to shine on Cup Final day. I remember as a kid it was always a special day, no matter who was playing. FA Cup final day was a television ritual: watching the teams at their hotels, interviews on the bus, *It's A Knockout*, wrestling... Sadly, it doesn't happen now – it's treated just like any other match, really.

But we were buzzing that day. Ray and me looked up at the stands as the fans began to stream in, the atmosphere boiling towards kick-off. I remember we talked about the pitch and how some teams complained it sapped their energy. Ray, who knew what it was like to win an FA Cup from his Arsenal days, just said, 'Only if you are getting beat.' One cool dude was Ray.

The joker in the pack that day, and every other day, to be

honest, was Terry McDermott. Back in the dressing room he stood up and did his spot-on impersonation of Bob Paisley – voice, expression, the lot – but always with one eye on the door just in case the boss appeared.

'Right, lads,' said Terry in his best County Durham accent, 'we've got this mob today. You know what they're like, man, they can blow hot and cold. Well, make sure they're blowing bloody cold, man!'

We were howling. Terry Mac should have been on the stage, he was that good.

I was the new kid, really – three days on from my twenty-third birthday – so I left it to the more experienced guys to ease the inevitable tension. And I was fascinated, watching Tommy Smith as our physio, Ronnie Moran, rubbed Tommy's chest and out would come a great loud belch. Just like me mum used to do to our Frank when he was a baby to get his wind up. Tommy said it was to prevent him getting a stitch in his side at the start of the game. Well, you learn something every day.

I sat quietly, trying to block everything out of my mind but the job in hand: winning the FA Cup. I didn't give a thought to the fact that come Wednesday, we would be in Rome, playing in the European Cup final. Say it now, all those years later, and I sometimes wonder at the importance of it all but back then it was one game at a time and I knew I could handle the pressure. It might have been my first full season, but I already had two league titles, a UEFA Cup and a Charity Shield win at Wembley under my belt.

The secret to achieving that level of success was being

able to cope with it all and we were good at that: we had played so many high pressure games to win the League and get to this final and then the European showdown the following week. All we had to do was keep it together for two more matches and we could write our own chapter in the club's glorious history.

So no, I wasn't nervous – quite calm, really, even though for me this was the big one, the top of my wanted list ever since those days in front of the telly with me mum. I wonder if today's professionals think the same way.

I looked round the dressing room at Emlyn Hughes, Kevin Keegan, Stevie Heighway, Terry Mac and of course there was big Ray Kennedy, who had already won the double with Arsenal. What was there to be nervous about? I'm not particularly superstitious either, just one little routine: I would always put my shorts on last and that would be just as we went through the dressing-room door. If you were going to have a superstition it had better be something you would never forget to do, I thought!

As the referee's buzzer went, all twenty two players plus subs clattered into the tunnel. There were some nods to pals, even one or two handshakes between familiar rivals, but that was not for me. I never shook hands before a match. That could wait until after the final whistle when, win or lose, I would shake everyone's hand.

As we lined up, my focus was totally on the game. I just had no idea what a bittersweet afternoon it was going to turn out to be for the team, and certainly for me.

It was United who got to play in their home strip but I

wasn't bothered. I liked our white shirt with that Liver bird on the chest, standing proud in Anfield red.

You hate the waiting before a big game like that. Blow the whistle and let's get on with it! But Wembley on FA Cup final day isn't like that; there are all the formalities to get through first, and slowly, the tension builds. Then we are on the move, Bob Paisley leading us out alongside Tommy Doc. As we emerge from the gloom of the tunnel, the sunlight is blinding and the noise rattles our eardrums.

We go through the formalities: a handshake from the Duke and Duchess of Kent, and some suit from the FA, then the National Anthem. Finally, we peel away to our respective ends, wave to the fans, kick a few balls. I'm ready. Bring it on!

Bob Matthewman, a good ref, gets it started and we quickly settle into our possession game, building from the back, looking to dominate in midfield. We push United onto the back foot, create a few decent openings; Ray heads against a post. But Buchan and Brian Greenhoff are colossal in defence for United and half-time comes with no goals.

Still, we're happy. The dressing room is buzzing. Bob and his coaches, Joe Fagan and Ronnie Moran, tell us that if we keep playing the way we have been playing, a goal will surely come.

Well, it came soon enough, but not the way we were expecting. The fans barely had time to pick up their pies and get back to their seats before Jimmy Greenhoff headed on a long ball from the back, Pearson gambled and picked the right number, and from the corner of the eighteen-yard box, he unleashed a fierce shot that seemed to surprise Ray Clemence.

What the fuck was going on here? All that good work and we're one down, only five minutes into the second half. It was against the run of play, but that can happen. What matters is how you react. Teams are always vulnerable just after they score and hard and fast, we came back at them. Within three minutes we were back on level terms.

I scored. Me, Jimmy Case, the so-called hard man coming up with a bit of delicate control and then an unstoppable shot from the eighteen-yard line. To this day people say what a fantastic goal it was, one of the best FA Cup final goals Wembley has ever seen... and in the next breath they ask me what the hell I was doing on the edge of the box, smack-bang in the middle of the pitch when I was supposed to be wide right.

Well, this is how it happened.

Throughout the first half I had been watching Kevin Keegan's movement, especially when our left-back, Joey Jones, got the ball. Kevin would jog along the edge of the penalty area and as Joey shaped to fire in a high ball, he would come short for a chipped pass.

So we're one down and I'm thinking I need to get more involved instead of staying out on the wing all the time. Stevie Heighway gets the ball at his feet and I drift towards the corner of the box, right behind Keegan. We're lined up like two planes coming into land at Heathrow. Steve passes to Joey and Kevin is off, jogging across the box, ready to pick up the expected pass.

Whether United had wised up to the move or what, I don't know, but the plan changed because Steve Coppell forced

Joey inside, onto his right foot, and anybody who knows Joey on his right peg, that ball is going nowhere near Kevin Keegan. I just knew he would find me instead... and true to my word, he over-hit the pass to KK.

I can see the ball arcing towards me as if in slow motion, right onto my thigh. It all happened in perfect harmony, with perfect timing. I cushioned it with my right, pulled the ball down and then pivoted like a frigging ballerina and lashed it on the half-volley. It was like a good drive on the first tee, right out of the sweet spot. Don't bother diving, Alex, no one's saving that. Top corner. 1–1.

Wembley erupted – well, the Liverpool end, anyway. I'm leaping up and down, Phil Neal wraps his arms round me, then raises his fist in triumph towards our fans. It's often been said that scoring a goal is as good as sex. I'm not sure about that but what I can say is that there is no feeling quite like it – the adrenalin rush, the euphoria, the noise, the excitement... I've scored in a Wembley Cup final... Get in, you beauty!

No question, it should have set us up to go on and win. United had held their lead for only three minutes, they should have been down and ready to be taken. We rolled our sleeves up and set about them but fate had decided to play a different hand.

Only three minutes more on the clock and United came up with one of the craziest goals ever seen at Wembley. It was a sheer bloody fluke. I have seen the goal about three times and every time it looks worse than the last.

It was a tackle-cum-shot from Lou Macari that was destined for Row Z in the stands when it hit Jimmy Greenhoff on the shoulder and deflected towards the goal and out of the reach of Ray Clemence. Three goals in five minutes and we were losing again. Unbelievable! The Liverpool fans filled Wembley with a tremendous noise as we tried everything to get back at United, but it was not meant to be. And I guess we knew it wasn't going to be our day when Ray Kennedy smashed a shot against the woodwork late on, with Stepney beaten all ends up.

We were still on the attack when Matthewman blew the final whistle. I can remember sitting down on the turf, having given it everything, believing we had been the better team, and feeling bitterly disappointed about losing. No, it was worse than that: I was totally gutted. And let me tell you, back then, losing at Wembley in the FA Cup final was a horrible feeling. That was the nature of the prize.

As I sat on the Wembley grass, deep in thought, Joe and Ronnie walked around, patting us on the head, trying to lift our spirits. There was another big game coming up and we had to be ready to go again. But right then I could only think about the disappointment of losing my first Wembley cup final. I thought about my family watching from the stands and there and then, I made a promise. Like Arnie used to say, 'I'll be back.'

It's funny how things turn out. I thought one day soon, I would be back with Liverpool. In fact, I never thought I would play for any other club; that I would be at Anfield for the whole of my career. But six years later, in 1983, I was back at Wembley, this time wearing the blue and white stripes of Brighton and Hove Albion on the final day of a roller-coaster season in which Brighton had got relegated... and won a place in their very first FA Cup final.

What a bizarre season that was. We struggled in the League, shipping goals by the hatful, but the FA Cup was different. It started with a win at Newcastle in the Third Round. And who am I up against at St James's Park? Only Terry McDermott and Kevin Keegan. You couldn't make it up. And that was just the start of a whole string of coincidences during that extraordinary run to the final.

On paper, we looked a decent side, with players like Steve Foster, Steve Gatting, Tony Grealish, Gary Stevens, Michael Robinson, Andy Ritchie and Gordon Smith. And to be honest, we weren't playing that badly, but the fact of the matter was that we couldn't string two league wins together. If anything, we were too open and at times defended like a Sunday pub team.

You can't play like that for forty-two league games and get away with it, especially at the top level, but in the Cup it's different. Half a dozen games, with a bit of luck along the way, and anything can happen.

We beat Newcastle in that replay at St James's Park, then we stuffed Man City 4–0, and that's when you start to get a feeling that it might just be our year. Back at the Goldstone Ground, we all crowded round the radio to listen to the draw for the Fifth Round. All we wanted was a home tie. Instead we got Liverpool away.

I mean, come on, play the game! Was Lady Luck taking the piss? Sending me back to Anfield, along with our manager Jimmy Melia, a Kop favourite in the fifties, to take on my boyhood favourites. So what had I done to upset the old girl? Ironically, the Liverpool team included central defender Mark Lawrenson, who had been signed from Brighton by Bob Paisley at the same time that he sold me for £350,000. And it turned out to be a special day in my life. I had had my fair share of unforgettable moments with Liverpool, but that day in February 1983, playing in the stripes of Brighton, is up there with the best.

Anfield was packed as usual for an FA Cup tie in those days. The Kop heaved and swayed, passion flowing from the terraces, which is always worth an extra man to Liverpool. But they were briefly silenced when we scored. Just after the half-hour mark Michael Robinson went through Liverpool's defence like a hot knife through butter and set Gerry Ryan up for a tap-in. Then came the inevitable siege and we held out until well into the second half, when Craig Johnston came up with this amazing bicycle kick to equalise. I reckon that's the best goal an Aussie has ever scored! The Kop roared and snarled, baying for blood, expecting the inevitable victory... but then I buggered it up for them.

There wasn't long to go and I was just outside the box when a clearance dropped perfectly onto my right foot. I didn't need a second invitation. Bang, back of the net! I have to admit I did celebrate the goal. I've seen players go back to their old clubs, score and then do the whole humble bit, but that's not me. I loved scoring goals and that was a biggie. Coming near the end of the game, it meant so much to Brighton, so no apologies for going off on one.

And the Kop understood. They knew, deep down,

Liverpool would always be my club but I was a Brighton player and I did what I had to do. When the final whistle went, the Kopites sang 'Oh, Jimmy, Jimmy' and I gave them a wave. Nice moment that, the sort of memory that stays with you.

Anyway, as I came off the pitch this TV reporter shoved a bloody great microphone into my face and said, 'This is Bob Paisley's last season. Do you realise you have just robbed him of his last chance to win the FA Cup, the only trophy he has never won?'

I gave him a stare and then said, 'What about me? I've never won it either. Do you think Bob Paisley would have lost any sleep thinking about me if we had lost?'

We drew Norwich at home in the Sixth Round and by then FA Cup fever was starting to grip the town. Just to put it into perspective: Brighton had never been in the quarter-finals before and despite the threat of relegation hanging over the club everybody was loving the Cup distraction.

To be fair, the Norwich tie wasn't much of a match: scrappy, littered with fouls, but there were a couple of incidents that have stayed with me. Second half, our captain, Steve Foster, who already looked like bloody Geronimo with his white headband, got an elbow in the head from John Deehan and went down in a heap. There was no rolling around, no one rushing up to the referee, trying to get Deehan sent off. Fossie just got up and carried on, his headband now stained bright red with blood.

The other incident of note came in the second half as well. We had just had a lucky escape when we broke away and I slipped through to score the only goal. Yeah, I certainly remember that. There was some doubt about the goal after the linesman raised his flag and then put it down again. Was I offside, had there been a foul? Did we care? Brighton were in the semi-finals of the FA Cup! Who would have thought it?

Norwich weren't happy, though, even after the referee later explained that the linesman's flag had been for a foul on me and he was just playing the advantage!

Ken Brown, the Norwich manager, had a go at me, saying I was lucky to still be on the pitch. Earlier, I had been booked for a foul and then I caught their lad, Mick McGuire. That got me a warning from the ref: any more tackles like that and I would be on my way to the dressing room. Never one to argue with officials, I had to tread carefully, but I don't agree with Brown. I had never been sent off before and it was not what you would call a dirty tackle; much worse went on.

After the game Brown said they'd been done by an old pro. Now, I rather liked that.

Four teams went into the hat: Brighton, Arsenal, Manchester United and Second Division Sheffield Wednesday. No prizes for guessing who we wanted to draw and we got lucky, the Owls at Highbury. For the fourth FA Cup game in a row I scored, another belter from outside the box after fifteen minutes. Wednesday equalised but late on Michael Robinson hit the winner and that was it: Brighton were at Wembley for the first time in the club's history.

The town went mad. Down in The Lanes every shop window was dressed in blue and white; tickets sold out in minutes. I had been to Wembley many times with Liverpool, it was expected of them, but to do it with a club like Brighton was something else.

For the final, we did our bit in style. We flew up to Wembley by helicopter on the day and I suppose, looking back, it could have been a bit dicey. Most of the lads had never been in a helicopter before and that could easily have affected them. The last thing you want before an FA Cup final is a dickey tummy and a touch of the trots. But as we flew over the stadium, I looked around and I could tell everyone was up for the challenge. Bottom of the League, we were being written off as the biggest outsiders since Sunderland faced Leeds, but we had a real feeling we could win. It was a tough call, we knew. Our opponents, Manchester United, had finished third in the League, behind Liverpool, and we were bottom of the pile, a bunch of no-hopers. But underdogs always have their moments and it's what you do when they come along that matters. There is no doubt in my mind that not only could we have won that day, but maybe we should have won. Unfortunately, life is littered with could haves and maybes and no one is interested in hard-luck stories.

We went into the final with the same attitude that had got us there, to get in United's faces and be ready for the chance when it came. I don't know if we surprised them with the intensity of our play or if they were just not in the right frame of mind, a bit complacent, perhaps. Whatever, we started much the stronger and Gordon Smith deservedly put us in front with a far post header from Gary Howlett's delicate chip, a classic centre forward's goal heading back across Gary Bailey. We held that lead for the best part of an hour but the game suddenly turned when Frank Stapleton got the equaliser and then Ray Wilkins curled in a beauty from the edge of the box. Bit out of character for him, I have to say, but they all count. Three minutes from time I pulled a corner back to Tony Grealish and his ball into the box found Gary Stevens with enough space to park a bus. The United defence had gone AWOL and Gary just picked his spot to make it 2–2.

Extra time flashed by, both sides scrapping and scrambling on tired legs. I kept thinking, 'Just give us one more chance.' It came down to the final seconds. United were pressing for the winner and they left the back door open. This was it. I clipped a ball over the top for Michael Robinson. He only had Gordon McQueen to beat and when he cut inside, the chance was there – shoot! But he bottled it. Instead of shooting, he decided to pass to Smith, who was coming up on his right. Gary Bailey came charging off his line, made himself as wide as he could... and saved Smithy's shot with his trailing leg. Had it gone in there would not have been enough time for United to come back.

It has gone down in history as the moment Brighton lost the Cup, immortalised for Seagulls' fans by a piece of commentary that went, 'And Smith must score', but to my mind, Smithy did everything right... apart from not lifting the ball just six inches higher. If only he had dinked it over Bailey's trailing leg it would have been in the bottom corner. It's easy to say now, thirty years later, but in the heat of the moment, who can blame him?

But I knew that was it. You don't get many chances to win an FA Cup medal and ours had come and gone. We'd put everything into that game and when the replay came round a few days later, we had nothing left. United had got their act together this time and it was too easy. No one was very surprised by the 4–0 scoreline.

But in no way do I blame Smithy for not scoring what would have been the winner. Years later we did a radio show with Danny Kelly on TalkSPORT – me, Arthur Albiston, Gordon Smith and Gary Bailey – and Gary was right when he said that Gordon didn't miss, he saved it. And I'll tell you something else: if we could turn the clock back and have that moment all over again, there's no one else I would choose ahead of Gordon from those eleven players to try to convert that chance into the winning goal. No, not even me.

Although there was no way I could have known, this time there would be no going back. That was my last chance to get an elusive winner's medal. It would have completed the collection: four League Championships, three European Cups, UEFA Cup, European Super Cup, four Charity Shields, and there was the 1981 League Cup we won as well. They are treasured possessions and precious memories – not bad for a council house kid from Allerton.

But I have another, more compelling reason to look back to the day we lost that FA Cup Final and a wish that for once I could re-write history, because that was the day my world turned upside down.

It had begun with such high hopes. I had the Wembley tickets all sorted out for Mum and Dad, my brother David and his wife, and they went off to Wembley by coach with a load of other Brighton fans who were friends of ours while I went off to join the team for our helicopter trip up to London. We flew back after the game, feeling quite good about ourselves with the draw we had made with the mighty Manchester United. I made my way home to get changed for the civic reception. As I left the house, I gave Mum a kiss on the cheek and said, 'Goodbye, Mum, see you later,' and I left her sitting happily with a cup of tea and a slice of toast.

At the reception I didn't feel quite right, a bit peculiar in fact, and I remember thinking it must have been the effect of the game ending in a draw after that great chance for us to win it. I just felt weird and somehow I knew something was wrong. It unfolded when I headed home at the end of the banquet.

As I turned into my road I saw an ambulance at the top end. And as I got closer, I realised it was outside my house. I jumped out of the taxi and rushed into the living room. My sister Linda was there with Dad, both of them in tears. He told me Mum had decided to go to bed early and then, without anyone at her side, she had died in her sleep. My mum had always been my biggest fan, my best supporter, and when I heard that she was gone, it was the worst feeling anyone could imagine. Everyone was in a state of shock and disbelief. I remember turning to Dad and, thinking about the heart attack he had had years earlier, I said I had been more prepared for him to die before Mum.

It took me a long time to get over Mum's death. We were always very close and, as the months and years passed, and even to this day, I think to myself that she was only sixty-three years old. She had just retired and that was the time I was going to look after her even more, but I never got the chance.

I am sure you can imagine what it was like. We all sat round, drinking tea, not knowing what to do, and then the thought came that we had to get word to Frank, our youngest brother, up in Liverpool. We didn't want to tell him over the phone, or let him hear it on the radio, so first thing next morning David and I caught a plane up to Liverpool. As the taxi pulled into his street he was just coming out of his house to go and get the morning paper. He didn't know, and telling young Frank was the toughest thing I have ever had to do.

Mum's death at that age put everything into perspective. Success and the rewards that come with it are all well and good, but they don't amount to that much if the people you love aren't there to share it.

CHAPTER TWO

FROM THE BEGINNING

It would be daft to say I entered the world on 18 May 1954 with a football at my feet. Tell you what, it didn't take long, though. I was still in my pram, one of those big contraptions with shiny spoked wheels and a blue folding top, and my mum would proudly walk me down to Holly Park to see South Liverpool playing in the Northern Premier League.

We would roll up to the big gates where the team coaches used to go in and the men on the gate would open up for Mum to wheel me in. And we didn't have to pay because my mum's brother played on the wing for South Liverpool. His name was Ronnie Edwards but he was always known as 'Skinner' Edwards because he used to skin past all the full-backs he came up against.

I suppose Uncle Ronnie was my first football hero.

Now because my pram was one of those big old things set

on springs, it meant it was high enough off the ground for me to be able to see over the perimeter wall at Holly Park. I've been told that when the game started, if I wasn't facing the pitch I would start crying.

I was naturally the centre of attention – well, who can resist a toddler, even when the footy's on? Apparently, during the game my family and friends would come over to take a peek in the pram. I would get my cheeks pinched by the ladies while the blokes were talking tactics, telling me I had to be good with both feet, learn how to get a tackle in, and know how to head the ball properly. Some of it must have sunk in.

I grew up in a council house on Clavell Road, Allerton with my two brothers, David and Frank, and my sister, Linda. It was a terraced house in a block of four with a dark and narrow entry separating the middle two of the four houses. We three lads slept in one room, Linda in another. At first, we didn't have a telly but it was still a bit of a step up for my dad, David. He was a bit of a lad, was my dad. He came from Edgehill – Scorefield Street to be exact, but it's not there now. It was flattened years ago when they started to regenerate Liverpool and laid down a road to join the city up with the M62.

Scorefield Street was a typical row of terraced houses, just like you remember from those early episodes of *Coronation Street*. You had to roll up a copy of the *Liverpool Echo* and set fire to it to light your way to the outside lav.

Dad was one of seven brothers. His mum died early so I never got to know my gran, but Granddad got married again and produced another brood of children, finishing up with twenty-two to his name, and he lived to the ripe old age of ninety-eight. I don't know what he was on, but I wish I could get some.

It was a different world back then. I remember going down to his house with my dad holding my hand, I would be about four, and on the doorstep sat this bloody great big Alsatian dog. We stood about the same height and as I approached, it just eyeballed me all the way to the door.

In those days the front door of my granddad's house was open all day and all through the night, but he was perfectly safe. The Alsatian would be sat there and it would only let friends and family over the step. Anyone else it would bark to let the family know a stranger was outside. It was just like a nightclub doorman.

As Granddad sat there in his vest and braces, more dogs came running out: a Jack Russell and a whippet. In a cage in the backyard were two ferrets used by family members for poaching or ferreting for rabbits. Dad used to take my two brothers and me fishing or ferreting and we learned how to catch things and help put a good meal on the table. So we grew up on rabbit pie, pigeon pie and pheasant, if we were lucky. We didn't eat the fish we caught because in those times we were doing coarse fishing and you didn't take the fish away, just threw them back. But that didn't matter, I just loved the sport and I've loved fishing ever since.

Dad was pretty strict when we were growing up and laid down a simple rule: 'I don't mind what you do, just don't bring the police to the door.' He came from a big family and was determined to keep us all on the straight and narrow. I owe him a lot for the way I turned out.

21

He was a right character was my dad and when I think back to the things that he got up to, it was mad. Every year, a couple of months before Christmas, he would empty his shed in the garden of all his tools and gardening stuff and then lay down a layer of fresh straw. On the end of a piece of rope he would hang a feed hopper from the roof and then he would fill the shed with young turkeys. Dad always timed it so they were fattened up just in time for Christmas and then he would sell them down the pub to put a few bob in his pocket, always saving the best bird for our family Christmas dinner. Of course it had to be a big secret because the council had rules about keeping livestock in your house or garden.

He never missed a trick, did my dad. He worked on the railways and volunteered for the breakdown gang. That meant they could be called out at all hours if trains got into trouble but they would make a tidy profit if the trucks came off the rails and spilt their load. It would be the job of Dad and the rest of the gang to clean up whatever had been spilt but there would always be a bit of a divvy up among the lads when no one was looking.

I remember one morning getting ready for school, I went to the airing cupboard to get my clean vest and underpants and the whole thing was full to the brim with green, under-ripe bananas. Another time the sideboard groaned under the weight of Dairy Milk chocolate. We kids thought it was great and, growing up, it was just the norm in our house.

Mind you, Dad worked hard, all hours day and night. Sometimes he would be away for two or three days at a time if a derailment needed fixing. I remember as a kid coming home from school of an afternoon and the lads would start calling for me. Everyone knew Dad wa

used to put a woollen scarf over the do

would be hell to pay if my mates happened to w

Mum and Dad were married in 1947 and their fu

was one of those post-war council prefabs in Speke, right n

Evans Medical and the Metal Box. That's where our David and

Linda were born. It wasn't the best place to live but they had

to start somewhere and Dad soon set it up like Granddad's

house, with a wire fence right round it so he could have

chickens running loose.

Mum and Dad put their names down for a proper council

house and so when I came along they were nicely set up in

Allerton: Mum, Dad, David (who was seven), Linda (six), and

then Frank came along three years after me.

From the start I was football mad and I was made up when

I got a ball for Christmas. I was still only a toddler but as soon

as I could stand up for myself, I was learning to kick with both

feet and head the ball without closing my eyes.

I only ever supported Liverpool, and it always had to be

Liverpool, I never had any inclination to go over to the blue

side. Our house was red from top to bottom. I watched them

on television with my mum, who loved her footy (she had a

soft spot for Denis Law even though he played for United and

City, she said it was because he was a cheeky player). As early

as I can remember I was analysing games, watching what

different players did with the ball, where they stood and ran.

I went to matches as often as I could. Derby games, night

games in midweek, I would always be there. At first it was in

the boys' pen and then onto the Kop. You had to be fairly

robust to survive on the Kop. If you were right in the middle and needed to go to the toilet, all you could do was pee into a rolled-up newspaper. But there was nowhere better to watch Liverpool – Lawrence in goal, Chris Lawler, Ian St John, Gordon Milne, Willie Stevenson... What a team they had.

I can remember going on a school trip to Devon and Cornwall at the time when Liverpool played Leeds in the FA Cup final, in 1965. The radio was on and you can imagine the excitement of all the kids on the coach when the game went into extra time. Roger Hunt scored to make it 1–1, then the bus erupted as Liverpool took the lead with a headed goal by Ian St John. As the final whistle blew, we were all singing 'Ee-ay-addio, we won the Cup' over and over again. When you are a kid these are the telling times that make you want to be a professional footballer all the more, and even more than anything, to play for Liverpool.

My first school was Springwood County Primary School, a five-minute walk from home, and it was brilliant, mainly because it pushed everyone into sport. I always used to carry a tennis ball around in my pocket and any time there was a break, out would come the ball, two sides would get picked and we had a game. Tell you what, playing with a tennis ball doesn't half sharpen up your skills.

It was certainly a better idea than the time I tried to trap a 3 x 2ft concrete slab and broke four bones in my foot. I was about eight at the time and the council were doing some kerb repairs and had left these bloody great slabs lying about, so one of the lads in the street decided to move one. I'm just stood watching him and the daft sod dropped it on my foot.

24

They never put my foot in plaster, just put a splint on it. I was on crutches but after a short while I would discard them every chance I got and I was walking on it, playing with a ball and at one stage even trying to pole vault over a washing line in my mate's back garden! Anyway, when I went to see the doctor he took off the bandage from round the splint and it had snapped and just fell apart. He picked it up, threw it across the room and told me in no uncertain terms that I would never heal if I didn't take it easy. That was a good lesson I learned about injuries.

I also learnt about discipline. I used to get up to a bit of mischief and once got caught lighting fires in the churchyard. Afterwards I got the cane in front of the whole school at assembly, but the worst thing was I had to miss a couple of games of footy. That soon helped to straighten me out.

We used to pick sides and everyone wanted to be a Brazilian – Pele was the most popular, Jairzinho as well, but I always went for Tostão, a tough little midfield general – he was my sort of player.

Even in those days I wouldn't hold back. I didn't take any prisoners. It didn't always go down well with other parents but that didn't deter me from the way I thought the game should be played. I got used to being called a dirty little bugger.

There's a story that does the rounds that during a game between Garston Church Choir and the Allerton Scouts I gave the goalkeeper of the choir a hefty kick when the score was 23–22 to them! Honestly, I can't remember it happening, but it is a fact that I never did like losing.

I got spotted in the playground by the head teacher, Mr

Brian McDermott, and he asked if I wanted to try out for the school team. Of course I was made up to be asked and even happier when my mum and dad gave their permission.

I remember the shirt I was given – green and white quarters – and because I was one of the smallest players, the bottom of the shirt when tucked in would show below my shorts.

The school had a half-decent football team. Well, I was in it for a start, but so too was my mate John Gidman – he was the captain. John got into Liverpool's youth team before me, but he didn't get any further at Anfield. He did OK for himself, though, playing for Villa, both Manchester clubs and Stoke. Mind you, he also went to Everton – I always thought there was something strange about him! And he won a cap for England as well, which was one more than I got, but more about that later.

John also played for Liverpool schoolboys, something I never did. When I was fourteen I got sent for a trial and I went with high hopes because I'd read in the newspapers that so and so had got picked up by Liverpool, or Tranmere, or Wrexham, so it was a big opportunity and I thought I played quite well. I scored a couple of goals, but at the end of the trial I was told by the chap running things I wasn't wanted. His name was Tom Saunders.

Years later, when I had a trial for Liverpool, old Tom was then head of youth development at Anfield. After two weeks he came to tell me Mr Shankly wanted to sign me, but being a bit of a hot head in those days I said, 'Oh, you bloody well want me now, do ya?' hinting back to the day he turned me away from the Schoolboys. But to be fair to Mr Saunders, who became a bit of a legend at Anfield over the following years, he must have kept track of me after that school trial.

It happened again when I went for a trial at Burnley. By then I was playing for South Liverpool and I was turned down, this time by Dave Merrington. Years later I met him when I signed for Southampton after winning all those trophies with Liverpool. He was in charge of youth development and every morning if I passed him or came into contact with him, I would casually say, 'The one that got away, eh?' I kept that up for quite a few seasons!

Missing out on the Schoolboys' side was a real blow but I knew I wasn't big enough. I didn't have enough beef on me, unlike John Gidman, who was taller than me.

I loved everything about playing for the school, especially as we would get taken out of class if we had to travel to another part of Liverpool. To be in the school team was a real achieve-ment. Home games we would be in the changing room getting kitted up and then we had to walk across the playground to the pitch, everyone else watching and us all excited because we knew we were going to have a game of footy.

Even then I always had a decent hard shot from distance. I was only a pint-sized eight-year-old but I was asked to take all the goal kicks because nobody else could kick those heavy balls out of the eighteen-yard box.

We played on a full-sized pitch but because we were only little they used to tie a tape between the goalposts about halfway up between the goal line and the crossbar. Well, one year we got through to the semi-finals of the Schools Cup competition and there was all sorts of controversy when we got knocked out. I can't remember who it was we were playing but they got a corner and as it came into the box someone chipped it against the real crossbar. As the ball came down one of their lads tapped it in and the goal was given. We went mad because that crossbar shouldn't have been there!

After that, we were determined to come back, and we did. In 1964 Springwood won the Liverpool Schools Cup. Naturally, the school was quite proud of our great achievement and wanted to make the medal presentation a bit special so John Purvis, the dad of one of the lads in the team, used his contacts at Liverpool FC and managed to get Willie Stevenson and the legend that is Ian Callaghan to come along to the ceremony in the school canteen and present the medals.

We were all made up. Sandwiches, jelly and ice cream, permission to invite a girl from our year, and then going up to meet the star players! Ian Callaghan gave me my medal. Who would have thought that thirteen years later I would win the European Cup with him in the same side? It's funny how things turn out.

When I wasn't playing for the school, I would tag along with my big brother David when he went off to play on Springwood Park. Him and his mates were all big lads, about sixteen years old, and I would only be eight or nine at the time but I was always eager to join in.

First ones there would start practising until there were enough lads for a game, but because I was our David's little brother I would only get picked if there was an odd number. As soon as another of his mates turned up to even the numbers I had to sit down again.

They came from all corners of the park and as the numbers grew so the goalposts – made out of coats – would be pushed back to make the pitch bigger. I was up there every night and, looking back, I think I enjoyed those games because I loved the challenge of taking on bigger lads. Sometimes you would get knocked about a bit but that went with the territory and I soon learned how to look after myself, how to position my body to avoid bad tackles. It helped shape me into the player I would become and soon I was ready for the next stage in my career: mixing it with the dockers and pub sides from the toughest parts of Liverpool.

By then I was at Toxteth Technical Institute. John Gidman and me had gone our different ways after I passed the eleven-plus and he didn't. He went to the local secondary modern and I went to the high school. I'm not really sure how that happened. I mean, academically I was OK, but all I really concentrated on was football. I didn't have any other ambitions. If I couldn't be a footballer, I hadn't a clue about what I wanted to be. The high school was not as strong on sport as Springwood had been; it was more about academic achievements and study. Very strict, all the teachers wore gowns and that type of thing. We had to wear a uniform with a cap and when I started at Toxteth, I went to school in short trousers, which was not the best way to win friends and impress people. Mind you, I was only small but I had the piss taken out of me unmercifully. It all came as a bit of a shock after the fun days at Springwood.

The school was divided into four houses: Holt, Sefton, Stanley and Derby. I was in Sefton. We had inter-house competitions such as athletics, cross-country running, chess competitions, etc. I loved cross-country – I could run all day.

Our technical drawing teacher, Mr Ernie Gallagher, was right into his sport. He ran for the Liverpool Harriers and was a very good distance runner. He also formed a boys' football team (called Rogar) to play in one of the local leagues. We never had a boys' club or building, we just played football.

At Toxteth there was a lad with me called Paul Cliff – his brother Eddie played for Burnley at the time – and I always thought Paul was a better player than me and that he would get a pro club, but he didn't like the training side of things or the discipline of it. All he wanted was to have the ball at his feet and he was happy.

It just goes to show that all the talent in the world is no good if you don't have the desire and dedication to work hard and make the most of your ability.

I was obsessed with Liverpool at this time – going to matches, travelling away. Dad and me went down to London for a Cup game, at Tottenham. It was a fantastic, hard-fought tie, which ended 1–1. We brought them back to Anfield and Liverpool won the replay 2–1. Through to the Sixth Round, we drew West Brom away. This time Dad and me went to the match in his Mark 1 Ford Cortina. I can still remember the number plate – BLV 625B. It was another draw, and so was the replay. There were no penalty shoot-outs in the FA Cup in those days, so it was off to a neutral ground, Maine Road, Manchester. We lost the game 2–1 and it was a massive disappointment at the time because the FA Cup had, and still has as far as I'm concerned, a definite magic about it. So the chance was gone, but the memories survive of Dad and me going to the matches together. That was what football, and life, was all about when you were growing up.

When I got to sixteen, ready to leave school, my dad took me to one side and gave me a solid piece of advice: 'Get yourself a trade, son, and you should be in work for the rest of your life.' But what was I going to do? At that stage I didn't really think I could make a living as a footballer but I knew I didn't want to go on the railways, like Dad. I used to have to take his overalls to be washed and they were always filthy. And my brother David, he was a railway engineer and he would come home with his hands all covered in oil. I didn't want that. My first application was for a job as an office boy at the Liver Building, but I didn't get that, thank God, so I started work as an apprentice electrician at Evans Medical. A few years later, Dad passed on exactly the same advice to my younger brother Frank, who got an apprenticeship as a plumber, so he wasn't daft – with one son a plumber and the other an electrician, he had the house covered for repairs!

I was playing at weekends and starting to get known around the area. One Sunday morning I was in bed when I heard little pebble stones being thrown up at the window. I opened it and saw this bloke from up the street, Frankie Flynn, and his mate, Gerry Towie. They were chucking tiny stones because they didn't want to wake Dad up – they knew they would get slaughtered.

Frankie and Gerry were going to watch the Blue Union Stevedores and Dockers Social Club team play under the bridge, down Window Lane in Garston, and they wanted me to go with them. I was just putting my head back in the window when I asked, 'Do you want me to bring me boots?' They said, 'OK, bring 'em along.' I didn't get a game that day, but I was asked to sign for the Blue, in the Liverpool Sunday League.

That was a very, very tough league. The Blue were rough as arseholes but they were the best team in the area. When I got in the side I played on the right. The team had Tony McLaughlin, ex-Everton reserves; and Johnny Moore, a technically gifted lad. I often wondered why some of those players didn't make it. Then there was a fella called Tosh Jones, built like a brick outhouse. A massive bloke, his physical strength was unbelievable. Nobody messed about with Tosh. Everybody knows him around the area, even today.

One of my first games was on Sefton Park against East and West Toxteth, another rough outfit. Sixteen years old, I had just started work and I was up against raw-boned blokes who were well skilled in the dark arts of local football. It was a priceless education. One game, I got the ball and went to take on this big, grunting full-back. Just as I was getting past him the centre-back came across, a big ugly lad with thighs like tree trunks. I had already beaten him once or twice but he dived in, took the ball and me with it. We both slid right into the crowd, standing two to three deep on the line, and bowled them over like skittles. There were three or four of them lying on the ground and as we were getting up, it was as if a dark cloud had come over. I looked up and there was Tosh Jones standing over the both of us. He stared down at the centre-back, and said, 'You do that again and I will have you.' Tosh was the nicest bloke you could wish to meet, but he was also the team's minder and he had a bit of a reputation. Anyway, I didn't see the centre-half come anywhere near me again.

I learned a lot at the Blue. If you were going to survive you had to grow up quickly, learn how to look after yourself and never over-react. The coaches would say things like, 'Make your first tackle count, it's you or him that comes away with the ball', and something like, 'You have to earn the right to play', and that meant winning your personal battle with the player you were up against.

The words 'intimidation' and 'dominance' come to mind. I can remember playing against Burnley at Anfield and their Welsh wizard of a winger, Leighton James, lined up for the kick-off. My full-back just behind me on that day was a chap called Tommy Smith. Just before the referee blew the whistle to start the game Tommy shouted, 'Hey Casey!' and Leighton's ears immediately pricked up. I said, 'What's that, Tom?' and Smithy shouted, 'You flick him up and I'll fuckin' volley him!'

'Alright, Tom,' I replied, and sure enough, the first pass that came to Leighton he was so busy looking for Tommy and me, the ball rolled right under his foot and out for a throw-in.

That's the sort of thing I learned at the Blue. It was exciting, a challenging game of football. I was just sixteen to seventeen years old, up against thirty-year-olds, but that was everything I was looking for. They had a cracking side and just to be picked for the Blue meant you weren't a bad player. It was a very close-knit community down there and to play for them was like a badge of honour.

My style of play developed at the Blue and soon I began to get a reputation around the area. I could tackle, had good control, a good range of passing and a ferocious shot from any distance. Opponents soon knew that come a 50–50 (or even 60–40) tackle I wouldn't pull out, even if it was likely that one, or both, of us would get hurt. I had no fear, I didn't mind the pain – in fact I actually quite enjoyed it, especially the thought that the other guy was probably in just as much pain as me.

I had this high threshold when it came to pain, which meant I could take just about anything that was thrown at me, get up and walk away. And I never looked back, never picked the other guy up or shook his hand. I don't do 'sorry'.

I always thought that if you displayed any kind of contrition, you were just showing everyone in the stadium and, more importantly, the referee that you were guilty. On the other hand, if I got kicked or caught with a good one, I wouldn't blame the other player, I would just say, 'Well done... but just watch out!' Then I would have a right go at myself for getting caught.

I guess my attitude got me noticed. They saw someone who could play a bit and never backed down or gave an inch. I was ready for the next rung on the ladder. At that time South Liverpool, who were semi-pro and in the Northern Premier League, were starting a youth team, managed by a fellow named Alan Hampson. Gerry Towie from the Blue was involved and he was instrumental in taking me to South Liverpool.

They trained Tuesdays and Thursdays and played Saturdays. In the first team, if you got a win, you would get something like two quid in your boots in a brown envelope. I was on a four-year electrician's apprenticeship at Evans and I think I was on £11 10s a week, which I had to tip up at home to help pay the bills. If you could supplement your wages by getting into the South Liverpool first team it was well worth the effort.

The main entrance at South Liverpool was at one end of the ground and as you walked down the side of the pitch, on the halfway line was an old, small wooden stand and that was where the changing rooms were. I will never forget the communal bath that we all jumped into after a game or a training night. Just next to the bath was a massive boiler and every now and again it would play up. There would be rumbling sounds, then a loud bang, and all the lads would jump out and then get back in when it settled down. Most of all I remember the floor of the bath. It wasn't tiled but it was like rough gravel cemented together. As you sat there any sudden sideways movement and it would slice into your flesh. And as if that wasn't bad enough, the floor of the bath got so hot it could take the skin off your arse!

On the opposite side of the pitch was a covered terrace the full length of the pitch. It was about five to six terrace steps deep and immediately behind that was the mainline rail track from Liverpool Lime Street to London Euston. The trains used to thunder past and the whole terrace would shake. On a good few occasions the team would train under that terrace and thinking back, all the steps were corroded away, leaving a crumbling surface of dust tracks and rubble all the way along. That was where we used to do some sprints and turns. It was bloody treacherous! All it would have taken was for me to put a foot in a hole and that could have been the end of my football career.

My mate Peter Eales was in the team – he was the goalkeeper and mad as a box of frogs. He used to have a laugh and a joke with the supporters behind his goal while the game was on, even enjoy a crafty fag while we were up the other end trying to score. One game, he was leaning on the post having a chat and a smoke and not really concentrating. Suddenly this bloke says, 'Hey, watch out, Pete, they're coming.' 'Oh, shit!' said Pete, threw his cigarette down and raced to the edge of the area to make this great save at the centre forward's feet. He then kicked the ball clear, turned round, picked up his cigarette and carried on chatting as if nothing had happened. What a character!

Around that time – 1972, I think – I took my last penalty. It was in the final of the National Sunday League, against Aigburth Legion at Holly Park. I remember the game well because there was a big crowd and it was 2–2 at the end and we had to go and take penalties. And I remember taking my kick and as I recall, I hit it hard and it just scraped the outside of the post and went behind. I wasn't the only one to miss but we were beaten and after that I never took another penalty. It's the sort of thing they don't let you forget. Years later, there was a piece in the *Liverpool Echo* under the headline 'The Day Jimmy Was Put On The Spot' and even a photograph of me putting the penalty wide. The thing that strikes me now, looking at that old picture, was the number of fans crammed behind that goal – they must have been ten deep. Football daft, they were.

Things moved quickly for me at South Liverpool. I was playing in the youth team, just on seventeen years of age, when I went over to Burnley for that trial; a lad called Dave Griffiths and me. We drove over in his dad's car but after three days we were both told by the coach, Dave Merrington, that we weren't good enough. As I always tell parents of lads who are trying to get into the professional game, there will always be disappointments. It would have been easy to walk away from it, but you just have to have faith in your own ability and not give up at the first knock-back. After all, it was only Merrington's opinion and as it turned out, he didn't know as much as he thought.

But I knew he was right about one thing: I was too small and I had to do something about it. My sister Linda's husband, Ian Forsyth, worked at Lockheed in Speke and they had a gym so I went in there to build myself up and broaden my shoulders. I started to get the six-pack and, as I tell kids, that's the time you can shape yourself for the rest of your life.

Finally I managed to force my way into the first team at South Liverpool, but it had been a struggle. The team was a bit of a clique and I was getting frustrated at not being given a chance in the first eleven, so I went in to see the manager, Alan Hampson. I took a recent match programme with me, placed it on his desk and pointed to certain players and said, 'I'm better than him, him and him, and if you want me to play there, I can.' With that we had a good chat and I came away having got it off my chest. It wasn't long after that meeting that I got into the first team.

I had a run of games, about ten or a dozen, but any thoughts I might have had of playing for Liverpool I kept strictly to myself, until one particular night that sticks in my memory. It was a match against Matlock Town at Holly Park. A cold, wet, sleety, shitty night, and we were a goal down. I had mud in my hair, on my face, in my ears. You name a part of the human body and I had mud clogging it up. I was just about to take a corner when this bloke came walking past. He was wearing a flat cap and had a Jack Russell dog on a lead. He stopped and said, 'Alright, Jimmy?' I glanced at him and said, 'Alright,' thinking, 'You're under the stand and I'm out here in the pissing rain, do I look alright?'

We were 2–1 down, I was cold, wet and caked in sludge and, much as I enjoyed my football, at that moment a warm bath followed by a cold pint was all I was looking forward to.

I was about to put the ball down to take the corner when he said, 'Hey, Jimmy, would you like a trial for Liverpool?'

Seventeen years old, I was playing non-league footy on the sort of night when you wouldn't put the cat out and I honestly thought he was just a spectator taking the piss.

'Fuck off, will ya!' I said before firing that rain-sodden ball into the centre and forgetting all about him.

It turned out that bloke was Tom Saunders, the very same man who had turned me down for the Schoolboys, who was scouting for Liverpool at the time.

Tom was the man who fixed it for me to go to Anfield for a trial. Thank God he didn't take offence!

CHAPTER THREE
WELCOME TO ANFIELD

On a grey spring morning in 1973 I walked into Anfield, feeling ten feet tall. Here I was, walking through the gates of that great old ground where I had watched my heroes from the terraces. Liverpool legends like Gerry Byrne, Gordon Milne, Peter Thompson and a certain Tommy Smith.

I was there to play, albeit on trial, with the chance of signing for the mighty Liverpool: my team, my dream. Who would have thought it, eh? I was given a quick guided tour by Tom Saunders and I don't remember being nervous, perhaps just a little over-awed. I mean this *was* Anfield, the cathedral I had attended as a supporter, offering my prayers for a Liverpool victory. This was the place I wanted to be and, as we walked down the steps under the 'This Is Anfield' sign, I remember walking towards the hallowed turf and being told by Tom that I wasn't allowed on the pitch. Then he added, 'But I am sure your time will come to step out there and perform.'

It was then I found out that the scout who had spotted me in that game against Matlock Town was the very same Tom Saunders, but I suppose they had been watching me for a while. He fixed it up with Alan Hampson, the South Liverpool manager, and about a fortnight later, he called me in and told me Liverpool wanted to take me on trial. Bloody hell, Mum would be pleased!

I gave up my two weeks annual holiday and a trip to the Spanish sunshine to go and prove myself, although it didn't really occur to me then that perhaps this was my last chance to make it as a professional. After all, I had been turned down for Liverpool schoolboys and told by Burnley I wasn't good enough. What if they were right? Three strikes might have meant I was out. At the end of the day I could always go back to South Liverpool and those dingy changing rooms, dodgy boiler and that sloping pitch that dipped so much you couldn't see the winger from the opposite end. I'd got my job at Evans and I was earning enough money to save up for a car and a mortgage. If you want to look at it like that being turned down again wouldn't have been the end of the world, life would go on. But I have to admit I had always thought how nice it would be to earn my living playing football, and not to have to get up every morning and clock on. Now I had the opportunity to make it happen.

On that first morning at Anfield I was put in the away team dressing room to get changed. That was always where the club apprentices and the young professionals got ready, but then everyone got on the same bus for the ride to the training ground at Melwood – first team players, reserves and us kids. I watched and waited to see where the big lads like Tommy Smith, Kevin Keegan or Emlyn Hughes sat. Last thing I wanted was to sit in someone's seat and then be told to 'fucking move' in front of everyone.

I had also made my mind up about one thing: I wasn't going to change the way I played. Right from an early age my way had been to get stuck in, win the ball and not give it away cheaply. I see all these experts talking about different formations, about running the channels and playing in the hole, and just think they are trying to make a simple game difficult. Barcelona got it right: when you have got the ball, pass it to a team-mate, and when you lose it, get it back as quickly as you can. Teams would turn up to play Barca and fall back behind the halfway line, giving them the ball and letting them play. Stands to reason with the players they've got, eventually they will find a way through. My game was all about pressing and that was how I would play, take it or leave it.

Watching Tommy Smith, I learned a lot about aggression and tackling. And I liked his approach to the game. I would watch one of his crunching tackles and there would be a beaming smile on my face. 'Get in there, Tommy!' Just from watching him, I vowed to myself never to pull out of a tackle because, if I did, I would be letting Tommy down, not to mention the fans on the terraces. I wanted them to know that when I went in for a tackle I didn't worry about getting hurt, I was prepared to take one for the team. That's what it was all about at Liverpool – win the ball and then give it to another man in red. It was never about Tommy or Emlyn or any individual, it was about the team. That's what I believed then, and that was how I was going to play.

It certainly worked. At the end of the trial Tom Saunders called me into his office and said, 'Mr Shankly would like to sign you.' That's when I made my infamous 'Oh, you bloody well want me now, do ya?' remark. But Tom didn't even blink – he had heard and seen much worse in his time. He just repeated those golden words, 'Yes, Mr Shankly would like to sign you'... and I said no!

Can you believe that? My first reaction was to turn down Liverpool's offer of a professional contract from Mr Bill Shankly, no less. My mates and brothers thought I must be mad, but the truth was I still wasn't sure if I was good enough and I remembered what my dad had told me about getting a trade. By signing for Liverpool, I would have had to give up two years of my apprenticeship at Evans. What if I didn't make the grade? I couldn't go back to the apprenticeship then, it would be too late. So I said no. I guess it was a measure of how much Liverpool wanted me that they worked out a deal to take over my semi-professional contract with South Liverpool – for a fee of £500 – which would mean I could carry on with my electrician's job and play for Liverpool at the same time. Happy with that, I put pen to paper and became Liverpool's only semi-professional player. I had gone from playing football for £2 in the back pocket to a two-year contract with Liverpool on decent money, and I still had my other job on the go.

Evans Medical agreed to let Liverpool have me two

mornings a week, and pay my wages for that time. It worked out just brilliantly and I have to thank my boss, George Gange, who was over all the electricians in the factory. I'm not sure what would have happened if he hadn't agreed to the deal with Liverpool. Every now and again George would call me into his office. I would go in, wondering what I had done wrong, but it was always just to have a chat. He would ask how it was going with the football and the factory and I would tell him everything was just fine.

Monday mornings I would clock on at 8am, and then clock out an hour later, drive to Anfield, get changed with the rest of the squad and then it was off to Melwood for a morning's training and back for lunch. While the rest of the players were done for the day, I would clock back on at Evans from 2pm to 5pm. Tuesdays I would train with the schoolboys in the evening, Wednesdays I was at the Old Swan Technical College from 9am to 7pm, Thursdays was a full day's work and then training with the kids in the evening, just to keep my fitness levels up; Fridays I would clock on and clock off, and after a morning's training I went back to work. Hectic, but I was loving it.

Not long after I had signed as a semi-pro I was picked to play in the A team against Manchester United at their training ground, The Cliff. We had Kevin Kewley, Dave Rylands, Derek Brownbill, Brian Kettle, Derek McClatchey and Tommy Tynan in our team; all lads like me who, at that time, were trying to progress up to reserve team level.

Well, games between Liverpool and Man U, no matter which teams are playing, are always competitive with a few tackles flying about. On this day, just before half-time, our winger, Derek McClatchey, caught one of their players with a bad one. Derek got booked but on the touchline the coaches were arguing. Man U wanted him sent off, while our boys were sticking up for Derek. Then, out of nowhere appeared United's manager, Tommy Docherty, who had been watching from the pavilion. He started bleating out instructions to some of his players to get after Derek and do him. It just so happened that my dad was standing next to Docherty and he just remarked that it wasn't a very good example to show to the youngsters. Docherty lost his rag and let Dad have a volley of abuse. Now those two started going at it, hammer and tongs, and I know my dad was just about to fill the Doc in when the security guards stepped in and Docherty had him escorted from the training area. And a good job he did too because Dad wouldn't have held back.

Down at Evans there were a couple of electricians who I got on with particularly well, Joe Woods and Cec Roberts, two great blokes who brought me through my teen years, always taking the mick, having a laugh but still getting the work done. It was my job to make a cup of tea and we would sit down at lunchtime with a pack of sandwiches and have a chat. Joe once turned to me and said, 'How's it going at Anfield then?'

'Not bad,' I replied. 'I'm enjoying it and I'm learning all the time.'

'Bit like here then,' Cec said with a chuckle and then he asked, 'When's your next game?'

I told him we were playing Manchester City Reserves that night at Anfield. Cec and Joe put their heads together and then said, 'You'd better get your head down then, you will need all your energy for the match.' So I climbed up into this massive loft space in the factory that everyone called 'The Void' and the lads promised to fetch me if the foreman, a really decent bloke named Roy Gunn, ever showed up. From that day on, every time I had a midweek game with the Reserves, the lads would send me off for a couple of hours' rest. It really helped and I have never forgotten their friendship.

I played two seasons in the Central League for the reserves, one season under Ronnie Moran, the next under Roy Evans. We won it both years. There was a real mix of players. I remember Peter Spiring, Dave Rylands and Hughie McAuley at the start, but they soon left for other clubs.

Then there would be a bunch of first teamers just coming back from injury or not in the side and needing games: Chris Lawler played a fair few games, Alec Lindsay, Terry McDermott, Phil Boersma and even Tommy Smith. What a great opportunity that was for me as I tried to base my game around his example.

There was also a hard core of players that made up the nucleus of the side. I played 37 times one season and there was Kevin Kewley, Brian Kettle, John McLaughlin, Tommy Tynan and Alan Waddle.

I loved playing and I loved training. Every morning after we had gone through all the set drills, we would finish with a practice game. The coaching staff, Bob Paisley in goal, Joe Fagan, Ronnie Moran, Reuben Bennett, Roy Evans, Tom Saunders and Mr Shankly himself would be in one team and they would play against the kids. And everyone knew that if the coaching staff was losing, we would be going past the time to go home, but if they were winning then everyone would get to go home early.

I always used to get picked for the coaching staff and so did Ray Clemence. He loved scoring goals so he played up front. Bob Paisley would always wear gloves and any shots that came in, he always punched them away, double-fisted. I remember once being in the gym at Melwood when Bob came in, pulled on these leather gloves and set to work on a punch ball hanging from the ceiling. He had the technique all right, punching the ball with his right hand, and on the way back he would hit it with his right elbow, then with his left hand and left elbow. He kept this up for about fifteen minutes, got a real rhythm going, and then he finished, pulled off the gloves and walked out, muttering to himself. Not much of a conversationalist was Paisley.

One practice match we were playing, someone on our team got fouled. Shanks called for a penalty but the kids argued the toss so Shanks spots Chris Lawler, who was well known for hardly ever saying a word, walking round the side of the pitch and he turns to Chris and says, 'Hey, Chris, do you think that was a penalty?' And Chris said, 'No, I don't think it was, boss.' Shanks looked at him with daggers in his eyes and said, 'Chris, you've been here for ten years and don't say a fucking word and when you finally do say something, it's a fucking lie!'

I loved it. For me the whole place was magical and in my eyes Shanks was like a god. He was a unique character.

Tommy Smith told me this story about the time Shanks went off to Europe for a few days on a scouting mission and when he arrived back all the lads were up at Melwood, waiting for the boss and his back-room team to come in and discuss the next day's opposition.

Shanks was leaning over the tactics table and he started to say, 'Well lads, we've got West Brom tomorrow,' and at that moment he glanced up at the players, spotted Gerry Byrne and said, 'Hey you, son. What's that?'

'It's a beard, boss,' replied Gerry.

'Son, there's no fucking beards in my team! Shave it off.'

Then Shanks paused, looked at Gerry's glum face and added, 'Anyway, son, why cultivate on your face what's growing wild around your arse?'

The next day the beard was gone.

Sadly, I never did get to work at first team level with the great man. Come the start of my second season in the reserves Mr Shankly suddenly announced his retirement. I think I was in the town centre when someone told me. The first thing I said was, 'Fuck off, you must be joking!' It was a bit of a shock to say the least and with me still without a first team game to my name, I did wonder what might happen. Everyone was stunned, looking for reasons why, and a lot has been written about Mr Shankly falling out with directors and stuff, all of which might well have been true. Looking back, it was at the time Liverpool first had a sponsor's name on the shirt – Hitachi. I don't think that would have pleased Shanks because he was red, red, red all the way. I think he could see big changes coming and he didn't like the look of it. Can you

49

imagine him with a player's agent, for instance? He would have had them up against the wall by the throat.

I don't think he ever really wanted to retire. His biggest problem was that after he had finished, he couldn't let it go. He used to come back and walk round the training ground, even join in the five-a-sides we had. It must have been difficult for Bob Paisley because all the players still referred to Shanks as 'Boss'. But eventually he had to stop coming down. I suppose it got a bit embarrassing, especially for Bob. I think Mr Shankly found it hard not being involved on a daily basis... so then Shanks started to visit Everton's training ground on some mornings. Can you believe that! He couldn't get away from the game. Even Shanks's house overlooked Everton's training ground; from his bedroom window he could watch their first team put through their paces.

And who would have bet that the man to take over from him would be Bob Paisley? Here was a bloke who didn't like conversation. Usually, the most you got out of him was 'Alright then?' But tactically, he was a genius and he had this knack of instilling belief in you, just by a single comment. He always had time for everyone, for him it was just a natural thing. As far as I was concerned, nothing had changed. Bob simply built on Shank's foundations. He was an ordinary, working-class bloke and that was how he was going to run Liverpool Football Club. I will give you one example of what that meant.

Under Bob Paisley the atmosphere was always like a typically northern working men's club, with no room for fancy Dans. There was an occasion when Watford were at Anfield and their chairman at the time was Elton John. Wandering into the boot room, he asked for a pink gin. He was given a bottle of pale ale.

But I wasn't complaining: this was my world and I felt right at home. And I made it my goal to take everything in and do everything that was needed to become a Liverpool player. Although a quick learner, I was still a semi-pro, still nowhere near a spot in the first team, not even sure if I was good enough. I thought I was doing OK, playing pretty consistently, but I sometimes wonder if they didn't put me into the first team earlier because I was still semi-pro and I suppose there was the chance, in their eyes maybe, that I would just walk away. But that was never going to happen. I was there for as long as they wanted me, although there were a couple of occasions when I thought it might be a short-term relationship.

As I have said, the coaches used to like to get their boots on in practice matches, and one time we were playing when the ball bounced up between Ronnie Moran and me. I went in hard for the ball and we clashed, shin to shin, bone on bone; no pads. Anyone who has played the game will tell you it hurts. Like I said, the pain didn't bother me but it certainly hurt Ronnie. He jumped up and suddenly we were eyeball to eyeball. 'You're not playing fucking alehouse football now, you know!' yells Ronnie, and I just did my usual thing, turning my back on him and walking off, but with the nagging thought that perhaps he would have it in for me and might even turn the other coaches against me.

It's at times like this that you need a bit of something about you, a bit of steel to take the criticism, shrug off the bollockings and carry on. I've always had that, the mental strength to face disappointment and challenges. That's the kind of player I was and I couldn't change, but I wasn't sure if Ronnie was too impressed.

Then came the day I clashed with Alec Lindsay, another stalwart Liverpool player who could be a bit tasty in the tackle, and it proved to be a turning point for me. There was a gap in the fixture list so Joe Fagan and Roy Evans sorted out a practice game, Joe running the first team and Roy Evans with the reserves. We were all in match kit to make it as full-on as possible. For the first team it was not much more than a run out but for us reserves it was a chance to impress the coaches.

I was put out on the right, up against Lindsay, who I can best describe as a big, hairy-arsed full-back. He had played more than a hundred and fifty games for Liverpool, but I was determined to beat him. First time the ball came to me, I turned to go past him and he gave me a little nudge, just to let me know that he was the man and he wasn't interested in putting it all on the line in some practise match against a raw reserve who hadn't been near the first team. Joe and Roy were refereeing the game but not really bothering about any fouls so the next time I took Alec on he went in a bit harder, as if to say, 'Right, that's enough, don't come again'.

Anyway, third time I came at him he whacked me and the old red mist descended. I picked myself up off the floor and chinned him with a good right-hander and suddenly all the players were pitching in to hold us apart. Joe shouted, 'Alec, you walk that way to the left, and Jimmy Case, you walk that way to the right. The rest of you go back and get a cup of tea.'

The next day I was called into Joe Fagan's office and I really thought I was in for the chop. Joe sat me down and told me in no uncertain terms that I had lifted my hands and struck another player. He ripped into me, telling me that if it had been a real game I would have been sent off, leaving the rest of the players to soldier on a man down. 'Imagine if you did that in a European Cup tie – unforgivable!'

It was the worst bollocking I had ever had and I felt like a piece of shit, especially as it came from someone like Joe Fagan, for whom I had the utmost respect. He told me to clear off and get my head down and I took everything he said on board. If I couldn't learn from him then I might as well pack it in. I can honestly say that I never raised my hands again and I was never sent off for Liverpool. Oh, and Alec and me kissed and made up.

Many years later I was talking with Roy Evans about the old times and Roy said, 'Do you remember the time you chinned Alec Lindsay?' I laughed and told him I thought I would get the sack for that one. 'Not a chance, son,' he said. 'Joe just said, "That Case boy, he's got some aggression, hasn't he? I think we'll have some of that."'

If that was an important moment, another came one night in Uglys nightclub, which used to be on Duke Street in Liverpool and was a favourite hangout of the first team players. I thought it might be a good idea to try to mix with them a bit so one night I went down with a mate and sure enough, standing at the bar was Steve Heighway, John

Toshack, Phil Boersma and Tommy Smith. Bold as brass I walked up and said, 'Anyone want a drink?' despite the fact that I only had a fiver in my pocket. I reckon they realised I didn't have much cash, I mean I was still only a semi-pro, so they all said, 'No thanks', all of them except Tommy Smith. 'Thanks, lad, get me half a beer.' That couldn't have worked out better. Tommy was my all-time Liverpool hero and, from that day on, he became one of my best mates.

I also started to make an impression on the coaching staff and most of the time it was positive. They seemed to like my aggressive style… but it wasn't all plain sailing. I remember one match in those early days, half-time arrived and Ronnie Moran came to me, wanting to know why I was ignoring him. He said, 'I've been giving you a bollocking for most of the half for not dropping back.' I told him I hadn't heard him: 'You'll have to shout louder!'

It wasn't until years later, when I had gone to Brighton, that the truth emerged. People were forever telling me I had the TV on too loud so, finally, I went to get my hearing checked and the doctors discovered I had a growth on a bone in my ear which was causing partial deafness. From that day on I have worn a hearing aid, except for when I was playing. I don't think it harmed my football in any way. In fact, I've always maintained that it helped make me more aware of what was going on around me, especially if some-one was coming in for a tackle, because I could never hear anyone shout 'man on'!

I signed full time for Liverpool in May 1974. It had been two years of hard graft, working during the day, playing for the reserves, training in the evening and having to fit in night school. But I got through, became a fully qualified electrician and then put that to one side as I set my sights on trying to make the breakthrough into the first team.

The way to go was to give 100 per cent every time I pulled on the shirt, no matter where we were playing or who we were up against. Too many players put it in one week and then take it easy the next, but I could only play one way. As I listened to the coaches and learned my trade, I was just itching to get the chance to play for the first team.

In my first season in the reserves I played about thirty times, more than that the second season. I knew I was getting noticed, especially after I scored a hat-trick against Bury in a 7–1 win. I'd heard one or two around Anfield had started to compare me to the great Roger Hunt because I had a hard shot in my locker. I was trying to model myself on another Liverpool giant, Ian Callaghan, but there was one drawback... Cally was too nice, so I settled for trying to copy the top man, Anfield iron Tommy Smith.

When Liverpool got to the 1974 FA Cup final to play Newcastle we were all invited down to Wembley to be part of the big day, to soak up the atmosphere. It was an easy win, 3–0, and after the game it was off to The Savoy in London. The Cup was on the top table, the players were all laughing and joking, and right then I said to myself, 'I'm going to have some of that.' I wanted to be a part of it, not sitting on the fringes, but right there in the middle. I wanted to be a Liverpool player with winners' medals, trophies, all the glory... But I had to wait, nearly a year, for my chance. To be fair, I wasn't the only one. David Fairclough was a regular in that reserve team, along with a lad called Tommy Tynan, who went through that season scoring goals for fun. I thought he was sure to get a call up, but it never came. Tynan didn't play a single game for Liverpool and was sold on. He made a name for himself down at Plymouth Argyle and last I heard he was still there, driving taxis.

We would get a taste of first team action on Anfield match days when we were allowed to stand and watch from the little boot room. This wasn't the famous boot room where Mr Shankly and the coaches worked their magic, but further down the corridor, just to the left of the steps where you go down and touch the 'This is Anfield' sign. It was there to store our training boots for everyday use during the week, and on match days in case any of the players on the pitch needed some boot work – it saved them having to run all the way back to the proper boot room.

It was only a little room, about six feet long by about four feet wide. On match days sometimes, one or two up-and-coming reserve team players were told to go into that room and take in the atmosphere and tension as both teams arrived and walked down the corridor to the changing rooms. The whole idea was for you get a feel for what that area was all about, ready for when it would be your first time to get off the team bus and walk the walk to the dressing room on match day. From that vantage point you could see past the first team dressing room door, down the corridor to the players' entrance and the car park. Our instructions were simple: soak up the atmosphere but keep out of the way.

There was an old boy called Henry who worked at the club, always very smartly dressed on match days – suit, tie, overcoat. During the week, it was his job to do all the little but essential tasks, such as putting the big bath on for the players after training. On match days he had to make sure the communal bath was just the right temperature – a few degrees too hot or cold would mean a right bollocking from the players.

He had another job on match days and that was to let Mr Shankly know when the visitors' coach had arrived. As soon as the coach pulled up, off Henry would trot to tell the boss that the visitors were about to get off the bus and make their way to the away team dressing room. I loved to stand and watch as he and Mr Shankly came walking down the corridor, Shanks as usual with his suit on, shiny shoes, white shirt and the famous red tie. With Henry at his side Shanks would stop, put his hands on his hips, jaw jutting out, and eyeball all the opposition players as they walked past. What an awesome sight! Not until the last one had gone into the dressing room would he turn and walk back to his office. It was that intimidation factor at work again.

On another occasion when I was in that little boot room we were playing Manchester City and, as usual, our lads were first to arrive and walk down the corridor and into the home team room. About ten minutes later the City squad arrived and as usual Henry shuffled off down to Mr Shankly's office to let him know. Shanks came up, took up his position and eyeballed all the City players as they turned left into their dressing room.

I was standing just a yard away as the last player went in and then Shanks turned to Henry and whispered something to him. I couldn't hear what he said but with that, Shanks went into the first team room and Henry just wandered off. No one was supposed to disturb the opposition team between the hours of 2pm and the 3pm kick-off time but at about 2.15pm Henry appeared from nowhere, carrying a load of toilet rolls. I was still watching as he knocked on the City dressing-room door and one of their coaching staff opened it. Henry handed him the toilet rolls and said, 'Mr Shankly has sent you these because he reckons yer all crapping yerselves in there!'

It was a wonderful place to be a part of but I desperately wanted my chance to show him that I could do a job for him, not just for one match but every week. Before every match I waited for the team sheet to go up and then I turned away in disappointment when I saw no mention of Case J. on the list. I got a couple of trips as thirteenth man but that was even more frustrating. In those days there was only one sub so you didn't bother getting changed; you were there just in case someone fell ill before the match.

Still, there was a silver lining to that particular cloud. Thirteenth man picked up the same first team bonus as the players. I was on decent money, about £300 a week at that time, while the first team were on £150-a-point bonus so a victory for two points doubled my wages. I was able to buy my first car. It was a Mark II 1600E Cortina, registration TKF 673H, and I found it at a farm in a place called Burscough, just on the outskirts of Liverpool. It was in an old barn, covered in dust, but when I cleaned it up, it was a beauty: silver with a black vinyl roof. It cost me £600, quite a bit of money in those days, but it suited me. I was never that bothered about cars, unlike some of the players. Tommy Smith had a yellow Lotus Esprit, Terry McDermott had a Fiat sports car and Kevin Keegan had a big Datsun sports car, but that kind of thing really wasn't for me. I had a Ford Capri sponsored by Skelmersdale Motors and so did Phil Thompson, and I still drive a Ford to this day.

But the funniest was Alan Kennedy and Phil Neal, who were sponsored by LADA. The rest of the lads would joke that of a morning you could hear them coming from about five miles away. Those big, heavy motors had no power steering and one time the gear stick came out of its socket in Alan Kennedy's hand!

But cars never really interested me – all I wanted to do was play football. Trouble was, in those days there was very little shift in the playing personnel, unlike today with thirty players in a squad and all this rotation business. Barring injury, the team usually picked itself, so all I could do was make sure I was always ready, just in case I got the call. But as the 1974/75 season drew to a close it looked like my debut would have to wait until the next time... and then, out of the blue, it happened.

They say you should be careful what you wish for, but for me that was the start of an eight-year magic carpet ride when all my wishes would come true.

CHAPTER FOUR

INTO THE
FIRST TEAM

It was Friday night and I had trained as normal in the morning. The last thing I'd been told before I left Anfield was that I wouldn't be needed for tomorrow's game, the final match of the 1974/75 season at home to Queens Park Rangers.

Earlier in the day, up at Melwood, I had stood with the rest of the lads waiting for the team sheets to go up for the first team, reserves and juniors. I'd been playing regularly for the reserves that season, I think I made thirty-seven appearances, and I have to admit I thought there might just be the chance that I could get a shot at a first-team game as it was the last match of the season, with nothing at stake. What better time to give me a try? But my name was on the reserves list as usual and so I trooped off to the showers, grabbed a spot of lunch at Anfield and then went back home to relax.

I wasn't too surprised, or disappointed. So far I hadn't had a look-in so I didn't really expect to be involved at that late stage. I just got off home and, at about 6.30pm, I was sitting down at the kitchen table for my tea with Mum and Dad when the telephone goes and Dad walks into the hall to answer it. Dad comes back into the kitchen and says, 'It's Bob Paisley. He wants to know if it will be OK for me to take you up to the team hotel for about 8pm.'

'Why, what's up?' I asked and Dad replied, 'Bob never said.' Bloody typical, I thought, but I was nodding like a donkey so Dad just said, 'OK, Mr Paisley, will do.' That started a bit of a panic. Mum quickly ironed one of my shirts while I got my match day suit ready. My tea was left on the kitchen table as I rushed out of the door with Mum trying to calm me down and shouting 'Good luck' at the same time.

The first team always used the Lord Daresbury in Warrington in those days, even for home games. It was about a half-hour drive from our house, so I had plenty of time for thinking as we rolled along in Dad's old Cortina. I had been thirteenth man before so that seemed to be the most likely scenario but I thought perhaps someone could have been taken ill and I might just make it onto the bench as sub. What a good end to the season that would be.

Dad dropped me off at the hotel and the first people I saw were Joe Fagan and Ronnie Moran but they more or less blanked me. They told me to get a bite to eat and then get myself off to bed. I slept OK, but I was up sharpish next morning and it was when I went down to breakfast that I found out that Brian Hall was sick. Now you don't wish harm on anyone, but Brian was holding down the position on the right of midfield while I was playing in the reserves and as they say, it's an ill wind that blows nobody any good. As I got on the coach with the lads – Smithy, Kevin, Terry Mac and the rest – I have to confess my mind was working overtime again, just wondering what the chances were of getting a game, my first game.

Then the coach arrived at Anfield and we were straight into the first team dressing room. This is how I remember it unfolding. We all sat down, waiting for Bob Paisley to announce the team, me being the most anxious man in the room. It all started to sound very familiar, 'Clem in goal, back four of Smith, Thompson, Hughes and Neal, a midfield trio of McDermott, Callaghan and Cormack. The forward line is Toshack, Keegan and Case!' I had stopped breathing, I'm sure my mouth must have dropped open. I stood there wondering if I had actually heard him say, 'Toshack, Keegan... and Case.' Then Bob Paisley throws the number nine shirt to me and says, 'Alright, lad, see if you can handle that one!' And then the players are slapping me on the back, the coaches are saying, 'All the best, lad', and it finally sinks in that it's really happening. This was the day I had dreamt about almost from the first time I kicked a football.

My instructions were simple: stick to the right-hand side, do what was needed defensively and, when we had possession, get forward to join up with John Toshack and Kevin Keegan. Just the sort of tactics I could understand.

I will never forget walking out into the corridor, under the 'This Is Anfield' sign. I had touched it many times playing for the reserves and never thought about its significance before, but at that moment I realised what it meant. It wasn't put there as a welcome to visitors but as a statement: You are here now and you had better be ready... and I was!

I reached up and touched it, then walked out onto the pitch on a scorching afternoon, the heat inside the packed stadium hot enough to suck the breath from your lungs. Liverpool had missed out on the title just a few days earlier when they lost 1–0 at Middlesbrough and Brian Clough's lot at Derby had picked up a point somewhere which was enough for them to be champions, so there was nothing much riding on that last match. But that didn't stop more than forty-two thousand fans squeezing into Anfield to wave their heroes off for the summer. As I looked round the ground, at the flags and scarves waving on the Kop, I did feel a few nerves, unusual for me, but it was only because I wanted to repay the coaches for having faith in me and I wanted to do it for my family, especially Mum who had supported me right from when I was a kid.

It was all a bit of shock for her and Dad. Before the game I just had enough time to go into the players' lounge and tell them that I was in the team. They were made up, the pair of them. Now they were sitting up in the stands, watching me playing for Liverpool, so yes, I *was* a little nervous. But as it turned out the game went pretty well for me. After Tosh put us 1–0 up, I got brought down in the box by the ex-Chelsea defender Dave Webb. Kevin Keegan scored from the spot and then five minutes from time I fired in a cross for Tosh to score his second. Two assists on my debut, I was happy with that.

My only regret was that it was the end of the season and I would have to wait three months to try to build on it.

I kicked my heels through that hot summer of '75, did a bit of fishing with my dad and kept myself fit, all the while hoping I would be picked again when the new season started. And the signs were promising. I got to line up next to my best mate Ray Kennedy on the first team squad photograph and funnily enough, the first game was against QPR, away at Loftus Road... but I didn't even make the subs bench. So it was back to the reserves, keeping my head down and working hard, just hoping another chance would come my way.

Liverpool lost that first game 2–0, then drew at home to West Ham: just one point from the first two games. Perhaps that forced Bob Paisley's hand because for the next match, a home game with Spurs, he had to leave out Ian Callaghan and picked me in his place. Cally was one of my heroes, but I knew I had to do everything I could to keep his shirt. There was another forty-two thousand strong crowd packed in for a cracker of a match. Spurs had a decent enough side in those days with Martin Chivers, John Duncan, Steve Perryman, Alfie Conn, Jimmy Pratt, Cyril Knowles and Pat Jennings in goal. We won 3–2 and in the sixty-eighth minute I thumped one past Jennings to score my first senior goal for Liverpool. I remember a newspaper cutting at the time that said the FA had been thinking of banning players from kissing and cuddling after a goal and there was me, being swamped and hugged by Emlyn Hughes, Peter Cormack, Phil Thompson and Terry McDermott! Another red letter moment for James Robert Case.

My head was spinning, but there was no chance of me getting carried away. Bob Paisley saw to that when he left me out again for the next match. I didn't know what more I had to do but it was just his way of telling me that players like Cally had been there and done it, week in, week out, and I had to follow their example if I was going to establish myself as a fully-fledged first team campaigner. But even if the boss hadn't made up his mind, it seems others had. I was still using the reserves dressing room to get changed every morning for training while the top players, known to us rookies as 'the big heads', all used the first team changing room. The two dressing rooms were only two or three yards apart, but to a reserve player that first team room seemed a million miles away. Then one morning I came out to get a pair of boots from the small boot room just as Tommy Smith came out of the big dressing room at the end of the corridor.

'Alright, lad, how you doing?' he asked.

'Sound, Tommy,' I said, pleased that this Anfield legend seemed to have taken a liking to me, had even taken me under his wing. Perhaps he saw a little bit of himself in this young, hard-tackling, no-nonsense Scouser.

In the next breath he said, 'Wait there a minute.' Now, when Tommy Smith says, 'Wait there', you wait there. 'Isn't it about time you were getting changed in our room?'

I wasn't sure what to say so I just sort of mumbled, 'Don't know, Tommy.'

With that, he shouted at the top of his voice. 'Hey, Moransco' – his nickname for Ronnie Moran – 'isn't it about time that Casey was getting changed in our dressing room?'

There was silence for a moment so Tommy shouted even louder, 'Can Casey change in the first team room?'

Silence again, and then Ronnie Moran, who also got tagged with the nickname 'Bugsy' after the American gangster, called out, 'Go on then.'

Tommy turned to me and said, 'Go and get your gear now,' so I went off into the reserves room and grabbed my clothes, shoes and everything and Tommy marched me the two yards to the first team room and pointed at an empty peg in the corner, between his place and Ian Callaghan's. 'You get changed there from now on,' he said.

There wasn't a pecking order as such but the arrangement of players' pegs had a meaning. As you came through the door and turned right it was Tommy Smith, Ian Callaghan, then me, Chris Lawler, Terry McDermott, Phil Thompson, Phil Boersma and Colin Irwin... all Scousers. Over the other side of the room were the foreigners: the English, the Welsh, Scots and Irish. Don't get me wrong, it was never an us and them situation, we all got on brilliantly, but it wasn't surprising there was a special bond among players born and bred in Liverpool.

We knew more than anyone what it meant to pull on the red shirt of Liverpool and the commitment that is needed to keep our fantastic supporters happy. Coming from Liverpool, I knew every time I went out onto that pitch I had to give 100 per cent. I knew I could never pull out of a tackle, even if it was 60–40 against and I was likely to get hurt, because I was representing them and they were my people. Even today, with so many foreigners in the game, it is important that Liverpool keep bringing through players who have the city and the club in their veins. I cannot think of another club where that bond exists to such an extent as it does at Liverpool. Give the fans everything, work your socks off, and they will stick with you, even when the going gets tough.

The only tension in the dressing room was between Emlyn Hughes and Tommy Smith. The fact of the matter was they didn't like each other and they never spoke. I really don't know what the problem was. You hear stories, of course. It might have had something to do with the boss making Emlyn captain instead of Tommy. I have never asked him about it but I have an idea that at the end of that season, as captain, Emlyn had to go in to see the manager and talk about what was needed for the next campaign. Apparently, Emlyn asked for 'two fast full-backs' in place of Tom and Alec Lindsay. If word about that had got back to Tommy you could understand him not being very happy.

I never really had a problem with Emlyn although there were one or two incidents that made me think twice about him. At the time when we were being sponsored by Adidas, a load of their T-shirts were delivered for the first team squad... Emlyn had the lot. Then, on his testimonial night, he gave me a decanter with six glasses – and four of them leaked! I reckon they must have been seconds he had picked up somewhere. But on the field, he was one hell of a player. Remember, they used to call him 'Crazy Horse'? Apparently, he picked up that nickname after he brought down an opponent during a match... with a rugby tackle!

Once I had been given permission to use the first team dressing room I would always try to be first in, just to make sure I didn't get in anyone's way when the rest of the boys arrived. Still not a regular, I certainly didn't want to get ahead of myself. I had to stay quiet and patient, waiting for my next chance and then be ready to grab it. As it turned out, it would be more than a month and six games before I got the opportunity, but Tommy's gesture had been a real boost to my confidence. I got picked for a home game with Aston Villa, again in place of Cally, and again I scored. That was two goals in three appearances, but I was still on the fringe of the team. Up to Christmas 1975 I barely got a look-in – a couple of games, a couple of subs' appearances – but Liverpool were on a good run, and I understood where the boss was coming from. Patience was the name of the game as far as I was concerned.

The real breakthrough came on a trip to Spurs and a 4–0 win, Liverpool's biggest of the season, with another goal from yours truly. That's when I finally cemented my place in the side, hardly missing another match after that, and I think we lost only two more League games all season but we did get dumped out of the Cup that year, in the fourth round, beaten 1–0 by a Roger Davies' goal at Derby County.

I will never forget it because after the match we went to the Midland Hotel next to the railway station in Derby for a meal. It's a solid-looking, old-fashioned place and we were given a gloomy private room with this great big dining table in the middle, where everyone sat around, feeling pretty miserable about being beaten. We were allowed to order a drink with the meal and because we were all more than a bit pissed off, for most of us it was just a half pint. It was at the end of the meal, we had finished our sweet or pudding, most of the lads had ordered a coffee and then came this really bizarre moment.

Into the room walked a waiter in full uniform, carrying a black tray, shoulder high. Right in the middle of the tray was one drink in a small liqueur glass. Bob Paisley spotted it and in that instantly recognisable accent, said to the waiter, 'Eh, son, what's that on your tray, man?'

The waiter, with a deadpan face, replied, 'A Cointreau, sir.'

With that, the boss stood up, looked along the whole table and asked, 'Who ordered the bloody Cointreau?'

There was deadly silence for not one of the players would own up to ordering the flash drink in front of the boss. After a few moments Bob turned to the waiter and said, 'Get the bloody thing back, man!' The only one not laughing was Stevie Heighway, because he was the one who had ordered it.

In fact, the lads were laughing about that one for weeks and even to this day when we get together someone will just come out with it, in Bob's voice, 'Who ordered the bloody Cointreau? Get the bloody thing back, man!'

I finished that season with twenty-seven appearances and six goals, but that was just the bare bones of what turned out to be an incredible time for the club and me. We were on a charge towards the title, the ninth in the club's history, but we were being pushed all the way by QPR. Come the last day of the season, they had finished with a 2–0 home win over Leeds and were a point ahead of us.

We had to go to Wolves in midweek so we knew exactly what was required: a point would give us the title on goal average, a win and there would be no arguments. It was just the sort of game that every Liverpool fan would try to get to, whether or not they had a ticket. In those days the Molineux dressing rooms were behind an iron fence, as in a schoolyard, with the fans walking past right outside. If you opened a window, they could hear everything being said inside.

The ground was packed to the rafters, every ticket sold and then some. I'm not sure what the official attendance was, but whatever they said, it was wrong. So many more had got in that there were even people sitting around the touchline.

About forty minutes before the kick-off someone spotted Phil Thompson's brother outside, so Thommo asked Bob Paisley if he could let him in so he could get through the dressing room and into the ground. Bob said OK, so there we were, just getting in the right frame of mind for such a big match, when Thommo's brother comes walking through... followed by about twenty more people. Bob just looked at Thommo and said, 'How many bloody brothers have you got?'

It helped relieve the tension because all the pressure was on us that night. Wolves were already relegated and had nothing to lose and with Molineux ram-jammed, they were able to play with freedom. And it seemed to work, especially when a mistake at the back let Steve Kindon in to give Wolves a first-half lead. Try as we might, we just couldn't break them down.

There was a mass of Liverpool fans packed behind one Molineux goal, raising the roof with the noise they were making, and we had only fifteen minutes left to turn the game around, fifteen minutes to win the title. QPR had the champagne on ice.

A situation like this calls for something a bit special. It demanded the calmness in a crisis that we possessed and also the awareness of how to retrieve such a situation. Some teams who were chasing a goal might look to one player to try to beat three men and score, or start hitting long balls into the centre, hoping for a break. That wasn't the Liverpool way. We just kept passing the ball, trying to create an opening, instinctively aware that we would eventually find a gap and get another chance to break them down. Our style had proved its worth many times. We used to score a lot of goals late on because we would keep passing the ball right to the end, even into injury time, because we knew the chance would come. And that was how it was at Molineux. You just don't change the way you play; if anything needs changing it would be the guys on the bench who would make that decision.

It was Keegan, of course, who would make the break-through. As the goal went in, the Kopites surged forward, tumbling over the advertising boards and onto the pitch. Mayhem. It took everyone – players, officials, stewards – a few minutes to get them back onto the terraces before referee George Courtney could restart the game. We still needed another goal to be clear champions, but you could see in the Wolves players' eyes they were gone. The combination of our relentless passing game and the power of the supporters had them reeling. Nine minutes later Toshack got the second and back onto the pitch came the fans; another delay. The final blow of that remarkable season came in the dying seconds when Ray Kennedy added the third. As the whistle went, the fans flooded onto the field, Ray was knocked off his feet and buried beneath a mass of bodies, and this time they stayed to carry us round the pitch on a lap of honour.

I remember after the game the TV cameras came into the dressing room and Bob Paisley, a son of County Durham, told them, 'I'm proud to be a Liverpudlian tonight!'

Imagine how I felt. Christ, I'd come a long way, from the Blue Union Stevedores and Dockers Social Club to the champions of the Football League. But there was a lot more to that season, many more reasons why I look back on it with so much pride and pleasure. I played in my first Merseyside derby, April 1976. Would you believe there were fifty-four thousand inside Anfield that day?

Growing up in Liverpool, you soon learn how important it is to win the derby, whether a Red or a Blue. You are just hoping and willing your team to come out on top. It's great when it happens, misery if you lose, so to have the chance to actually get out there on the pitch and do something about it was incredible. What I remember of my first derby was David Fairclough, our so-called super-sub, scoring one of the best goals of his career. There were three minutes to go, the score was locked at 0–0, when Davey picked the ball up out on the right and just ran at the Everton defence. They parted like the Red Sea, couldn't get a tackle on him and then, from this daft angle, he fired it across the keeper and into the far corner. I reckon they must have heard the roar in Manchester. You look back on moments like that and think about what might have happened if he hadn't done it. QPR would have won the championship for the first time in their history.

That was the same game Terry McDermott got sent off... and it was my fault. Well, I started it when I slid into a tackle outside their penalty area. I ended up on the floor with someone lying there with me. Next thing there were twenty players swapping handbags and the one who got caught was Terry Mac. But that was the sort of thing that happened in derby games, all part of the fun. The first ten to fifteen minutes were always spent laying the law down.

There would be other Liverpool-Everton derbies to come, with plenty of incident and controversy, and I will talk about them later but for now, that was my first one under the belt and a day I will never forget.

And just to complete the story of that first season, I also made my European debut. I had played abroad before, in an U-21 tournament in Dusseldorf. That was when I first had a passport, because I'd never been further than Cornwall on a family holiday before.

I got a taste for European football right from that first time, and I loved it. We won that tournament, the first thing I won with Liverpool, and it was great, bringing the trophy back to Anfield. So I was more than ready when I made my European debut in the UEFA Cup on a freezing cold, brass monkeys' night in Poland. Liverpool had already seen off Hibernian and Real Sociedad without my help, but now I was picked to play against Slask Wroclaw and I was relishing the prospect. But when we walked onto the Olympic Stadium pitch, it wasn't a pretty sight: it was bare, rock-solid and rutted. We wore special boots with short, pointy studs to cope with the conditions and we were up against a team backed by forty thousand fans. None of that fazed us, we were too good for them and won 2–1.

The second leg was at a misty Anfield on one of those wonderful floodlit European nights that have become part of the Anfield legend. I used to love those nights with the lights piercing the gloom and the crowd in full voice – they always seemed closer to the pitch and it was so much more intimidating for the opposition. It reminds me of a story I heard about a foggy night at Anfield, way back when the ref could see both goals from the middle, but the fans at one end couldn't see the goal at the other. Anyway, a roar goes up at one end as Liverpool score. 'Who scored the goal, who scored the goal, ee aye addio, who scored the goal?' chanted the Kop. 'Tony Hateley, Tony Hateley,' came the reply from the Anfield Road end!

It was all too much for Wroclaw that night but it was a night I will never forget. It went something like this: in the twenty-second minute Tosh produced a piece of skill out on the left that opened Wroclaw up. He slipped the ball to me just inside the box and I turned the defender, picked my spot and hit a peach of a shot into the corner. Eight minutes later, KK ran at the back four and as they retreated, he passed inside, I pulled the trigger and my shot went straight through the keeper's hands: 2–0. Finally, one minute after half-time the best goal of the lot. Brian Hall hit a shot the keeper couldn't handle and I followed up to knock it in from a yard for the hat-trick. And why was that the best goal? Because it was the hat-trick goal and I scored it in front of the Kop.

I don't know if it was that performance that caught Don Revie's eye, but in February 1976 I got my international call-up! Just twenty-one years old, I was included in an U-23 squad to travel to Budapest for a junior European Championship match against Hungary. To say I was chuffed would be an understatement. I was still trying to nail down a permanent place in the Liverpool team so to be picked for an England squad was a dream come true, but I didn't want to be just a member of the squad, I wanted to play.

We travelled to Hungary on a cold night in March for the first leg but I didn't get a kick as England lost 3–0. I watched England tip-tapping it about, frustrated by Ray Wilkins and Graham Paddon in midfield, nicey-nicey players, but England badly needed someone to get stuck in and knock the Hungarians out of their stride. I was a bit bewildered that I wasn't out there on the pitch.

Come the second leg, two weeks later at Old Trafford, England had to overcome a three-goal deficit if we were to get through to the semi-finals. This time I got the call and I had to pinch myself when I thought that only two years earlier I had been playing for South Liverpool and there I was, pulling on an England shirt! I cannot tell you how proud I felt to have those three lions on my chest.

There were thirty-three thousand in Old Trafford that night and we got stuck into them from the whistle, matched them for skill and spirit... but then we let in a goal on twenty-one minutes. It gave us a mountain to climb, but we hit back when Gordon Hill went on a good run and popped the ball across for me to equalise. From then on there was only one side in it. We battered them, but their goalie had one of those nights when he seemed to get behind everything we fired at him. Then, in the final 15 minutes, we almost pulled it off. I crossed for Gordon Hill to score and with five minutes left Graham Paddon made it 3–1. We just couldn't find one more goal in the time left and so the Hungarians nicked the tie 4–3.

I was gutted by the defeat but I still thought I had done OK and there would be more caps to come. That was the last international at U-23 level England ever played, and as it turned out, I never did get a call-up for the full England side.

When you look back at my Liverpool record – three European Cups, four League titles and all the other trophies we won, plus European Young Player of the Year – you would have to say I played my part in one of the most successful periods any English club has ever had and perhaps I was worth a go for the national team. I never gave up hope, even in the days after Liverpool; I clung onto the thought that my hero, Ian Callaghan, had been called up at the age of thirty-five. But it never happened.

There was one occasion when both England and Scotland were playing and I think I must have been the only Liverpool first team player who wasn't away on international duty. It was a very disappointing time for me. I was left behind to train with the reserves and I remember feeling like I'd been left out on a limb.

I have lost count of the number of people who have asked how many caps I won and they cannot believe it when I tell them I didn't get a single one. I'm still not sure why I never got the chance. It wasn't as if England were pulling up any trees at the time but I didn't even get a shot at the England B team.

I read somewhere that perhaps the thinking was that I was too robust for the international game, but every team needed a Nobby Stiles in the middle of the park. I know for sure that Liverpool would have gone back for Javier Mascherano, given the chance, and he has been a regular for Argentina.

And while my reputation was that of a hard-tackling ball winner, I liked to think I could play a bit as well. You didn't get into the Liverpool team if all you could do was tackle. I had a decent range of passing and I could get to the bye line and whip in a cross, which usually found its mark. I used to take that split second to look up and see where Kevin Keegan was standing, or pick out John Toshack towering over the defence like the Empire State Building. I get so annoyed when I see wingers hit the first defender. If you know that's going to happen, don't try to cross it.

The other weapon I had was a fearsome shot. Anywhere from thirty-five yards in, I knew if I could get it on target, it would trouble the keeper – or fly into the net. I'm often reminded that when I used to shoot and the ball whistled just past the post, it would sometimes lodge in the railings behind the goal and the opposition keeper would need a helping hand to retrieve it so he could take the goal kick. But none of that made any difference; it still didn't earn me a call-up from England.

At that time Ron Greenwood was England boss and he picked six Liverpool players in his squad for a trip to play Spain in Barcelona. I had to watch as Phil Neal, Phil

Thompson, Ray Kennedy, Ray Clemence, Terry McDermott and David Johnson set off, along with Alan Kennedy (who was in the B team) for a game against Spain B at Sunderland. And it didn't end there because Kenny Dalglish, Alan Hansen and Graeme Souness were all playing for Scotland.

It was around that time that someone asked Bob Paisley why England couldn't play like Liverpool when they had so many of our players in the international team. 'Simple,' replied Bob. 'It's because they don't play Jimmy Case.' Disappointed as I was, I never let it affect my performances. Ron Greenwood went with Steve Coppell instead of me and if that was his opinion, I had to respect it. My main concern was to play my best for Liverpool, but I cannot deny I would have loved to play for England.

Years later I was taking part in a veterans tournament in Mauritius of all places. There were about thirty ex-pros from all parts of the country invited and we all flew in to Charles De Gaulle Airport in Paris to meet up, ready to board the plane to Mauritius. But the flight was delayed and we were stuck there for five hours. It has to be said that five-hour delays, thirty ex-footballers and lager on tap don't mix. Let's just say we were all a bit the worse for wear when we finally got on that plane.

Most of us went straight to bed when we got to the hotel, ready for an early start the next morning and off to the stadium for the round robin tournament. It was boiling hot and towards the end of the day the lads were flagging, especially from the effects of that journey and beer the day before.

When we got back to the hotel the organisers got all the players together and said we could have a rest day the following day so we all got round the pool in our Speedos, splitting up into small groups and having a few chilled ones. I was with the likes of Steve Foster, Andy Townsend and Barry Horne, all lads from my Brighton days. In another group were the London boys: Kenny Sansom, the Stein brothers and a few from Chelsea and Arsenal. It was just what you would expect. Over the years the London-based players always thought they were better than us northern lads, coming from the big city and all that nonsense. Anyway, the London lads were having a trivia quiz and after a few minutes Kenny Sansom shouts over the pool to me in that London accent, 'Hey, Casey, how many fuckin' England caps have you fuckin' got then?' I had heard him clearly enough, but I blanked him at first and then shouted back, 'Sorry, Ken, what was that?' Again he shouted, 'How many fuckin' England caps have you fuckin' got?'

I knew he was just trying to take the piss but I said, 'What's that, Kenny?' and he shouted it out again so everyone could hear. I shouted 'Three' and stuck three fingers up as I lay back on the sun bed, a beer in my hand. Out of the corner of my eye I could see Kenny and his mates discussing this. If anyone would know about who played for England back then it would be Kenny because he was always picked. Anyway, after about five minutes he suddenly piped up, 'Hey, Casey, are you sure you got three England caps?' and so I replied, in my best Cockney accent, 'Sorry, Ken, I thought you meant European cups... now fuck off!'

My only international appearance was that U-23 game, but it came and went in a flash. More important at that time was Liverpool's charge towards the European Cup final. We were through to the last eight and a tie against Dynamo Dresden from East Germany. That was a tough round. We drew 0–0 in Dresden and brought them back to face 40,000 at Anfield, knowing we had to win because an away goal could let them sneak through.

I could have had another hat-trick. In the twenty-fourth minute, I nipped in front of their full-back to pinch the ball and scored. Already I had hit the bar with a pile-driver and after half-time I did it again. Then Kevin put us 2–0 up and we looked home and dry, but with about half an hour still to go, Dresden scored. There was a bit of tension in the air as another goal for them would have been enough for an away goals win and that would have been a travesty. The truth is, we were better than them on the night and we should have put it to bed long before the final whistle.

I've watched the highlights on YouTube and one thing that strikes me is how calmly we reacted after scoring. It might have been a big European game with a lot at stake, but it was still just a handshake and a pat on the back. None of this sliding twenty yards on your knees, dropping to the ground to be buried by your team-mates or those silly celebration dances. Call me old-fashioned, but I never went in for that kind of thing; nobody did at Liverpool.

There was a game at Bolton and Ray Kennedy was on one side of the pitch. I was on the other and I had got the ball. I looked up and could see Ray just coming towards the edge of the box and as he looked at me, he tapped his chest. I drilled a cross-field pass straight to him, he brought it down on his chest and then calmly stroked it into the far corner. All he did was glance over to me, wave to say 'Cheers' and then walked back for the kick-off. Enough said! What a player, what a great fella.

When the UEFA Cup semi-final draw was made in March 1976, we got Barcelona. Not quite the dominant force they became in recent years under Pep Guardiola, but still a formidable side. They had a host of Spanish internationals and two Dutch stars, Johan Neeskens and this fellow called Johan Cruyff. At that time he was the world's most expensive footballer and, as far as I was concerned, he was the best. His pace and creativity was so majestic with all those twists and the Cruyff turn, he was a joy to watch.

I knew all about this pair, having watched them in the World Cup, and I loved the way Holland played. What did they call it – 'total football'? The tag fitted and Cruyff was their standout player, of course. We knew we had to be on our toes if we were to get past them.

The first leg was at the Nou Camp, a vast stadium with the best facilities money could buy. We were surprised to learn there was even a chapel in the stadium but when you look at Barcelona's history, you realise religion is important to them. We walked round the place and when we came to this chapel, we went inside and had a team meeting. It was quiet and peaceful and we respected that, but it was a special time that helped concentrate our minds on the game ahead.

I will always remember Bob's team talk. He had a problem

remembering the names of the opposition so he had this habit of calling them 'doings'. Where that came from, I have no idea but at one point he said to Phil Neal, 'Hey, Nealy, the winger – er, erm... doings – he's not very fast, but he's nippy.' We surmised he was talking about Johan Cruyff. Then Bob lapsed into his days as a Desert Rat during the war and said, 'The left-back... er... errr... doings... he likes to go on a sortie... Jimmy, just stop him, will ya.'

Some of the lads had a vacant look on their faces but what Bob meant was that the full-back liked to get forward on the overlap. His way of describing it, as a 'sortie', was typical. He loved to drop in words and phrases from his days in the Army during the Second World War.

We were going into the lions' den, no doubt about that. No English side had ever won in the Nou Camp. It was an intimidating place, with seventy thousand fans behind them, towering over us from those skyscraper stands, and our contingent tucked away in a corner; it felt like the world was against us. But I looked around and saw Smithy with his chest pushed out, Emlyn geeing everyone up, super-cool Ray Kennedy looking like he was out for a game on the local park, and up front Tosh and Kevin. How would the Spaniards cope with them?

Not very well, if truth be told. Maybe Barcelona didn't take us seriously enough. Liverpool had won the UEFA Cup just a couple of years before but at that time we weren't one of the giants of European football and everyone south of Dover expected Barcelona to roll us over. So when John Toshack scored after 13 minutes it certainly shut the Catalans up. You could almost reach out and touch the stunned silence that descended on the Nou Camp. From that point on we played the game at our pace, knocking the ball around, restricting them to shots from distance, the perfect away performance.

At the final whistle I witnessed something I had never seen before. The Barca fans weren't just booing their team, they were hurling seat cushions onto the pitch in disgust. I don't think it helped the situation too much either when Joey Jones climbed out of the dugout and starting frisbeeing them back into the crowd. That's when Bob Paisley grabbed Joey by the back of his jersey and said, 'Get down the tunnel – you'll start a bloody war, man! They're not throwing them at us, they're throwing the cushions at their own players.'

It didn't take the Barcelona board long to react. They soon kicked the manager out of the door and by the time they arrived at Anfield for the second leg, they had a new man in charge and he had got them playing with a bit more freedom. There was still a huge task to face if we were to book a place in the final.

Now there have been some great European nights at Anfield but, for my money, never one to beat the night we took on Barcelona. The build-up was crazy. Everyone wanted a ticket and come match night, more than fifty-five thousand crammed into the ground, an attendance record that has never been beaten. Just getting into the place was a struggle, with hundreds more ticket-less fans on the streets outside, wanting to be around the place to share in the atmosphere.

The first half came and went in a blur. No goals, the tie poised on a knife edge. We had to get the first goal and just after the break it came. Tosh and KK finally combined to set up Phil Thompson of all people. He's still going out to lunch on memories of that goal, scored from way out – it must have been at least six inches! But unlike other sides that had come to Anfield and wilted in the face of our pressure and the fans' encouragement, Barcelona were made of sterner stuff and equalised almost straight away. Bob Paisley always maintained it was a goal they didn't deserve, but you have to give them credit. They showed some bottle that night but hey, I can say that now because we held on to win the tie 2–1!

I have to say it was a privilege to play against Johan Cruyff. He was the best I ever came up against. It was impossible to read what he was going to do. He'd push the ball one way and then go the other; stop and start when you were least expecting it. I wouldn't say he gave me a roasting, it wasn't really my job to mark him, but I did lose him on a couple of occasions. You just had to tip your hat and acknowledge you'd been done by a master. Still, they were going home to Spain and we were looking forward to a two-leg final against the Belgian side FC Bruges, with the first game at Anfield.

Bruges had never been in a European final before so that made us the bookies' favourite. Now I've never been a gambling man but I wouldn't put my money on any two-horse race in a cup competition. Bruges were an unknown force and we all know anything can happen in a cup-tie. I started on the bench and, like everyone else, I couldn't quite believe it as Bruges went 2–0 up inside twenty minutes. And it was no fluke. They scored with two well-taken goals and then gave a display of possession football and quality defending that had everyone scratching their heads. In the first twenty minutes they dragged us all over the park and created so many chances. For them to do that to our defence, in front of the Kop, was impressive. They were a damned good side.

But that was when Bob Paisley was at his best. He might not have been the most articulate manager in the history of the game, but his tactical nous was spot-on. As we left the bench at half-time to go down the steps towards the dressing room, he said to me, 'Get yourself ready to go on. We're not waiting ten or fifteen minutes, you're on straight away.' They had decided to take John Toshack off and as soon as I got in the dressing room, I got my shin pads and tie-ups on and I was ready to go.

It was going over and over in my mind that at any moment the boss, Joe or Ronnie was going to come over and bombard me with tactics and tell me what to do when I got out there. Don't forget we were 2–0 down at home. Out of the corner of my eye I could see them on their way towards me and I was already thinking tactics when they strode up and gave me my instructions: 'What we want you to do is go on and cause bloody HAVOC!'

The boss had decided to change things because Tosh had been getting no change out of the Bruges' back four. When he sent me on for Tosh it allowed Ray Kennedy to move further forward. It was a touch of genius – the Belgians couldn't handle Ray that night. He scored a blinder for the first, hit the post for me to bundle in the second and it was his pass for Stevie Heighway to win the penalty that KK converted for a remarkable 3–2 win. I've never heard the Kop in better voice; they inspired that tremendous comeback.

Thousands made the trip across to Belgium for the second leg and it was another nerve-tingling affair because Bruges scored first, from a penalty, and with their two goals at Anfield, they were ahead on away goals. But we soon got level on the night. Keegan scored it, and from that point on, we went into professional mode, keeping the ball, squeezing the life out of Bruges to take the trophy, our second of the season, with a 4–3 win over the two legs.

Nearly forty years on, sitting in my house on the outskirts of Southampton, a long way from the backstreets of Liverpool where I grew up, it all seems a bit unreal. Could it really have happened? I was just a local kid who had broken into the first team and in my first full season I had won the League Championship and then the UEFA Cup. Talk about Roy of the Rovers! Could it get any better than that? Well, read on... because it did!

CHAPTER FIVE

CHAMPIONS OF EUROPE

They had an uncanny knack of keeping your feet on the ground at Liverpool. Joe Fagan, Ronnie Moran and especially the boss, Bob Paisley, never let the players get too big for their boots, never let them start thinking they were better than they were. After that first season getting established in the first team, I was practically walking on air around Anfield. I'd played twenty-seven times alongside my heroes Tommy Smith and Ian Callaghan, mixing with the big stars like Kevin Keegan, John Toshack and Stevie Heighway. We had won the First Division championship and the UEFA Cup, I had scored a few goals along the way, and then, as the following pre-season unfolded, I played my first game at Wembley, in the 1976 Charity Shield final. There were seventy-six thousand there to see us take on surprise FA Cup winners Southampton and we edged it 1–0, with a goal from

Tosh. Within the space of twelve months I had gone from reserve team player to a European champion and Wembley winner. I couldn't wait for the new season to start.

We were working hard at Melwood, preparing for the big kick-off, and I remember this particular day, we had arrived back at Anfield for a shower and some lunch. I was walking down the corridor from the first team dressing room towards the players' lounge to get a bite to eat, just flicking my fingers through my hair as it was still wet from the showers, and not really paying much attention to who was around when I saw the boss come out of his office. He was heading for the treatment room, which meant we would have to pass each other. Bob didn't talk to me much in those days. It was nothing personal, everyone knows he wasn't a great talker and especially with the young players like Joey Jones and me, so I was prepared for the usual, 'Alright?' and walk on. But as we passed each other Bob said, 'There's one in there for ya.' I carried on walking, half-turned and said, 'Sorry, boss, what was that?' Bob was halfway down the corridor by now and he just repeated what he'd said, 'There's one in there for ya, in my office, go and get it,' and with that he disappeared into the treatment room.

What the hell was he talking about? I hadn't a clue so I just marched into his office and there on the desk, just lying in a jumble, were all these little black boxes with yellow Post-it notes stuck on the top. I could see one that said Ray Kennedy, another for Phil Thompson, Kevin Keegan, all the lads; and there was one with my name on it. I picked it up, ripped off the label and on the top of the box, written in gold letters, I saw the words 'Football League'. I opened it up and sitting on a piece of shiny silk was my League Championship winners' medal. It looked fantastic, varnished wooden background with a gold decorative plaque on top. This was what it was all about as far as I was concerned. But that was the end of it. I'd been thinking there would be a proper presentation night, perhaps with Jimmy Tarbuck, who is a big Reds fan, or Cilla Black, and each of us would go up, get a handshake from the star and be handed our medals. No such luck. It was just 'there's one in there for ya'. As far as the boss was concerned, that was history, put it on the mantelpiece, and let's go again.

Another time I was put in my place was one morning when I turned up for training at Anfield, all kitted up and ready for the shout for all the players to get on the bus for the trip down to the training ground. Then, just before we got the call, I was trying my training boots on and I snapped one of the laces. There was no way I could jiggle it about to fit so it meant getting a new pair. I rushed down to the boot room and knocked on the door. No one could just walk in – you had to wait to be invited in when someone opened up. It was a toss-up as to who would open the door, but I was hoping it would be Joe Fagan. In my eyes Ronnie Moran was the bad cop and Joe was the good cop. Well, you can guess who opened the door: bad cop Ronnie!

I said to Ronnie, 'Look, I've just this minute snapped me lace and I can't do anything with it. Can I have a new pair of bootlaces, please,' and he said to me, 'Have you signed your new contract yet?' I was a bit confused, what did he want to know that for? I said, 'What?' then added, 'Yes, I signed an extension last week.' Ronnie replied, 'In that case you can have a pair then,' and he went and got me some laces, and said, 'There you go, son.' In his next breath he shouted at the top of his voice, 'Right – let's get on the bus, you lot!' and away we went to training. Talk about not getting ahead of yourself. That was the atmosphere around the club with Joe, Ronnie and the boss.

Bob had his own way of getting things across to the players. He didn't particularly like team meetings or facing the press and as it is at all clubs, players would love to have a go at copying the boss behind his back. Terry Mac could do him to a 'T' – the facial expressions, the voice, his walk with the hint of a limp; Terry was good. We would all have a go at doing the boss, but Terry was the best. But it was never done with any malice, it was just us players having a bit of fun; we all loved and respected Bob too much for that. I will always be grateful for what he did for me and I wouldn't hear a word said against him. When Mr Shankly retired, there was a lot of speculation about who might come in. I have to admit that I, for one, was a bit worried in case some outsider arrived with his own ideas and didn't fancy my style of play, but when they gave the job to Bob everything just carried on in the Shankly style... except Bob made it even better.

He took us into the 1976/77 season on a mission: to win the European Cup for the first time. It had been Mr Shankly's ultimate dream to put Liverpool at the very top, and Bob Paisley was determined to make that dream come true. There were changes for that season. It was the first time we wore those famous V-necked shirts for a start. David Johnson had come in from Ipswich for big money but Kevin Keegan and my mentor Tommy Smith had both announced that it would be their last season. Keegan was looking for a move abroad and as for Tommy... well, time had finally begun to catch up with him and he was ready to call it a day.

I spent the first half of the season getting splinters in my backside from sitting on the bench, week in, week out, usually named as substitute and just itching to get into the team. It was hard for me to break in because Liverpool only lost twice up to December and at home we were near enough invincible. Bob was all for keeping a settled side so, once again, it was all about being patient and being ready. And then, briefly, the wheels started to come off. We only picked up two points in December and that disastrous run included a 5–1 thrashing at Aston Villa. I was sub again that day and it was like watching a horror show unfold as everything Villa did went right for them, while everything Liverpool tried went wrong. How could that defence of Phil Neal, Joey Jones, Emlyn Hughes, Phil Thompson, with Ray Clemence behind them, let in five? When the fifth one went in, Joe Fagan turned to me and said, 'What position do you want to play?' I thought he was going to send me on so I just said, 'I don't mind.' Then there was silence. After a minute he looked back and said, 'Jimmy, you stay where you are, son – they got themselves into this bloody mess, they can get themselves out of it!' What could I say, we were five down, so what difference would a sub have made?

Next match we were beaten again, 2–0 at West Ham. I was sub again. West Ham had a couple of lads who could dig in, Billy Bonds and Frank Lampard Snr, but they also had a lot of skilful, creative players. Trevor Brooking, Alan Devonshire and Pop Robson, I remember. Their problem was they sometimes went missing in games, but that day they were just too good for us. Brooking scored and their centre forward, a decent striker named Billy Jennings, got the other.

I always enjoyed trips down to London and I always wanted to beat the London sides. They fancied themselves too much for my liking, especially the supporters being from the big city and all that; they thought they were top of the pops and we were a bunch of louts from up north. Arsenal and Chelsea, they liked to mix it a bit, try some strong-arm stuff but we were always a match for any side when it came to aggression. Tottenham played all right at times, but never had the consistency to win the title as we were doing, season after season. As far as Spurs are concerned, I don't suppose much has changed over the past thirty-odd years. But the team I most liked playing against was West Ham because they tried to play the game the right way. They had a sign at their ground, similar to our 'This Is Anfield' board, which read 'Academy of Football'.

I remember one particular game in London, at Arsenal, when we were having our half-time cup of tea and team talk. A minute before we were due back on the pitch for the second half the coaches were telling the lads, 'At the end of the game get off the pitch as quick as you can, we need to get going quick to catch our train.' Well, you've never seen anything like it; all the lads ran off the pitch and ran through the showers, dried themselves and in minutes were on the bus. Bob was at the front of the coach, asking, 'Where are the bloody outriders?'

Anyway, they arrived and we were escorted to Euston station, flashing blue lights, the lot, and the bus went right

through and up to the track so we were able to
the train as it was ready to pull out. We just .
settled down in the buffet car with Ray Kenned,
sitting closest to the kitchen and bar. That's where we
sat and everyone knew that and would leave those seats fo. .
It was the same on planes: the rear two seats nearest the drinks
trolley were always left for Ray and me.

That day we had the buffet car to ourselves and permission
to have something to eat, plus a few drinks, on the club's tab.
Ray and me got chatting to the steward and tapped him up to
keep an ear on what Bob and the coaches were saying, up the
other end of the carriage. As we were getting near home, he
came and told us the boss had said there would be another ten
minutes and then he was shutting the tab. Just enough time for
Ray and me to order six more miniature bottles of Taylor's
1972 port!

We had got a taste for it by then so when we pulled into
Lime Street, Ray and me headed down town for a few more
drinks, ending up at Uglys nightclub. To be honest, there
were a few sessions like that, featuring yours truly and Mr
Kennedy, including some that didn't always end quite so
peacefully, but more of that later.

We were heading into the busiest time of the season, with
the FA Cup looming and European Cup ties to face. There
was a run of seventeen games in three months and, not
surprisingly, injuries started to pile up. At the end of
December, I got the nod for the game at Maine Road against
Manchester City, who were shaping up to be our closest
rivals for the title. That season, they had a decent line-up; in

goal was Joe Corrigan (we would eventually team up at Brighton and become good mates). They also had Willie Donachie, Mike Doyle, Dave Watson, Brian Kidd, Joe Royle and Dennis Tueart. A nice blend, with a winger named Peter Barnes sitting on their bench. We ended up drawing that match 1–1. It proved to be a vital result because we took the title by a single point, ahead of City, and I never missed another game.

The FA Cup run that season was fairly routine until we got to the semi-final stage and were drawn to play Everton. Everyone had been hoping the draw would come out differently and set up the chance of a Liverpool-Everton final, but it was not to be. Still, it would go down in history, certainly on Merseyside, as one of the most memorable, dramatic and controversial derby games ever played.

There was always excitement in Liverpool ahead of a derby, the atmosphere in the city was, and still is, electric, but the added spice of a cup semi-final – next stop Wembley – all hyped up by the media, pushed it up to fever pitch. For the fans it was massive. No one wanted to go into work Monday morning, having to face rival fans, knowing they would be going to Wembley; we had to win it for them.

The game was played at Maine Road and it was a mud heap; the rain was coming down in sheets, it was dancing down. Everton had been having a decent run and on the day they played well, perhaps better than us and maybe they deserved to win, but you don't always get what you deserve. We scored first. It was Terry McDermott at his best. He got the ball just outside the area and fooled a defender by dragging it back behind him with his heel, à la Johan Cruyff. He then had time to look up and chip the keeper from about eighteen yards.

Then Duncan McKenzie got the first equaliser for Everton. A talented player, Duncan, with loads of skill, but for me he was never a main man. He was flashy and had a bag full of tricks, but he was not a player of great consequence when you look back at his career.

There were about fifteen minutes to go when I put us 2–1 up with a looping header into the far corner. It had been a real melee in the box, with everyone up, and when I scored, I just got buried by the lads. What a moment! We all thought that was the winner, but with five minutes to go, Bruce Rioch equalised and then a replay looked certain.

What happened next, as they say on *Question of Sport*, is still talked about on Merseyside to this day. In the dying seconds of the game Everton's winger, Ronnie Goodlass, put in a cross and Bryan Hamilton bundled it past Clem. Everton thought they had won it, and so did we. But then everyone realised the referee, Clive Thomas, had disallowed the goal. Was he offside? Tommy Smith was pointing to where Hamilton was standing and he thought so, but when we all looked at the linesman he just stood there with his flag by his side. There was also a thought that Hamilton had handled the ball, although he claimed it went in off his thigh, and that was why Clive Thomas had ruled the goal out. I couldn't see, so who knows? All I can say is that the game finished 2–2 and we had been let off the hook.

There were mixed feelings in the dressing room afterwards. We knew we had been lucky and that Everton probably deserved to win the game but we also knew we had the chance to put things right and that it would be different, come the replay. And we were right. We went back to Maine Road in front of another fifty thousand plus crowd, with that nice Mr Thomas refereeing the game again. But this time we didn't give Everton a sniff. Three goals without reply, including one from me, meant it would be Liverpool heading for Wembley.

Evertonians still bang on about it to this day. That's why they are known as 'The Bitter' and, to be fair, Liverpool fans never lose the chance to stick the knife in. But it was more than thirty years ago, so get over it!

It's the same scenario with the Geoff Nulty injury saga. Everton fans still blame me for the tackle that ended his career. That was in the Merseyside derby in 1980 but, for the next ten years, even when I went back to Goodison with Brighton and Southampton, they always let me know what they thought. The abuse would rain down from the stands: 'Oh, Jimmy-Jimmy, Jimmy-Jimmy-Jimmy-Jimmy Shithouse Case'. I took it as a compliment. With them chanting that I knew I was playing well on the day, and had in the past, and I must have got right under their skins for them to hate me that much. Ah well, never mind, eh?

As far as I'm concerned, the ball was loose in the middle of the pitch, it was a 50–50 ball there to be won, and anyone who knows me knows I always went in hard. Anything less and that's how you get hurt. My knee smacked into his knee and it just so happened that my knee was stronger than his. No one likes to see any footballer's career ended through injury, but he wasn't the first and he certainly wasn't the last.

I have no regrets: all I was doing was my job, going in hard to win the ball, and he came off worst. It was a football injury, plain and simple.

But the fallout rumbled on. It would be about a year later, I had gone to Brighton by then and I was substitute, sitting in the dugout, when this chap in the crowd climbed over the wall and went to hand me this letter. I just put my hands down by my sides and so he dropped it right in front of me. Someone else picked it up and opened it. He had been trying to serve me with a writ from Geoff Nulty's solicitors, but I never accepted it. I got on to Liverpool straight away and they said they had also received one. They told me not to respond and after that it just fizzled out. I have never seen him since but Everton supporters still challenge me about it; I always tell them I had no intention of hurting Nulty, I was just going in for the ball as hard as I could.

When I meet Evertonians, I get a mixed reaction with half of them saying that I meant the tackle, and the other half saying, 'You did us a fuckin' favour there, he was crap anyway!' Then I say, 'If you want to talk about the time I had Graeme Sharp stretchered off, well, I meant that one, it was either me or him.' As far as I am concerned, it's all good banter with the fans.

After the semi-final the pressure started to build because that's when everyone started talking about the treble. Could Liverpool win the League, the FA Cup and then go on to win the European Cup? For us the worst thing wasn't the physical tiredness of playing so many games, it was knowing we were so close – and yet there was still every chance we could end up with nothing. I think that's where experience kicked in again. We had won the UEFA Cup the year before, we had won the Championship; we knew what it took, on and off the field. Most of the time all we needed was a good few pints after the game and anything that needed to be said was said and we were ready to go again.

I loved playing in Europe, coming up against different players, different styles and different challenges. It made you think about your game and how to combat theirs, how to score a goal against the sort of defensive formations you didn't face every week in the Football League. I relished it as a change from the weekly grind of the First Division. And for a Scouser who had only ever been as far as Cornwall on holiday with the family, it opened my mind to different cultures and I lapped it all up. Turkey was certainly an eye-opener. We were drawn against the Turkish champions Trabzonspor. I didn't play, but the trip was something to remember. How can I best put it? Well, Turkey was bloody awful! But remember, we are talking about more than thirty years ago, in the days when no one would have dreamt of going there on a package holiday.

We had been forewarned by our European spy, Tom Saunders. Yes, the same Tom Saunders who spotted me and who had been Anfield's head of youth development. If ever there was a man whose blood ran Liverpool red it was Tom. In his time he also worked as chief scout and ended up a director. But in those days he used to go all over Europe, watching the opposition, writing reports for the boss on the players we were likely to face and the tactics they used. This was before the days of video and blanket TV coverage so his job was vitally important. He also checked out the hotels we were staying in and, most important, the food. He came back from Turkey and announced that the food was OK, but they cooked it with gallons of oil and if you weren't used to it, it could easily lead to an upset stomach.

Bob was taking no chances. He recruited a chap called Jack Ferguson, general manager of the Holiday Inn in Liverpool, to come on the trip and oversee the kitchen when they were cooking for us. Just to be on the safe side, though, Ray and me took chocolate and a loaf of bread; Terry McDermott even brought along a couple of tins of sardines. The hotel wasn't up to much either. When Ray and me went to our room we checked the beds, they looked like they'd been knocked up from a couple of wooden pallets with a mattress thrown on the top.

On the European trips, if we had time, in the afternoon before the game we would always go out for a walk, looking around the shops. That day in Turkey, we were walking down this street not far from the hotel and we soon realised there were three or four lads following us. Then there were half a dozen of them. We went into a shoe shop and when we looked back, there must have been about twenty of them outside, arms round each other's shoulders, some even holding hands. We didn't know what to make of it, but the shopkeeper was able to make us understand that they were just inquisitive because they knew we were Liverpool players. That came as a bit of a relief, I can tell you.

It was all a bit unnerving, but nothing like the atmosphere that greeted us when we got to the stadium. That was down-right hostile. There were twenty-five thousand fans packed

into the ground and hardly any of them were from Liverpool
– it was such a difficult place to get to in those days. The pitch
was rough as a council tip, covered in stones, and the other
thing I remember was the distinct smell of garlic wafting down
from the crowd.

We lost the game 1–0 to a penalty, but we had seen enough
to know we would be able to take care of them back home. If
they thought we might struggle being strangers in a foreign
land, then running out in front of forty-two thousand at
Anfield certainly shook the Turks to the core. The 3–0 win
was a walk in the park.

I got into the side for the next round, against the French
champions St Etienne who, by most people's reckoning,
were just about the best team in Europe at the time, even
though they were having a poor run in their own league.
They were European Cup runners-up the year before, and
their team was full of French internationals plus an
Argentinian centre half named Oswaldo Piazza, who looked
like he could wrestle Giant Haystacks. For the first leg in
France we had KK out injured and Bob drummed it into us
to try to keep a clean sheet and if we could pinch an away
goal, so much the better. Well, we should have done. Phil
Thompson missed a sitter early on, heading wide when he
was unmarked, and Steve Heighway, who had their full-
back so confused he thought it was Sunday, curled a shot
against the post. Those misses looked a bit costly when St
Etienne got the only goal in the second half, but they hadn't
shown too much to worry us – well, except for a nasty
tackle by that Piazza bloke, which chopped Cally off at the

knees. Justice was done. Piazza was booked and that meant he had to sit out the second leg.

It was all set up for the return to Anfield and another of those unforgettable European nights on Merseyside. When I meet older fans they all talk about two great nights at Anfield: The European Cup semi-final in 1965 when Liverpool beat Inter Milan 3–1 and that game against St Etienne. It was another 55,000 sell-out, with the rest of the red half of Liverpool glued to television sets and radios. We took to the field with twelve men, if you can count about twenty-five thousand nutters crammed onto the Kop as an extra man. I have never heard or seen anything like it. The Kop was just a heaving mass of red and white flags, steam rising from all those cramped bodies, and they reckon you could hear the singing down by the Albert Docks. These days the Kop is all seated, with a lot fewer bodies in there on European nights and big games. They are still the driving force behind the team but in my day there could be twenty-eight to thirty thousand in the Kop, so I was so grateful to be out there on that memorable night to experience the unique atmosphere. It is something I will take to the grave.

It's hard to believe but the noise before kick-off got even louder when Keegan looped a shot over their keeper with less than two minutes on the clock. Anfield was rocking, but to be fair to the French lads, they didn't wilt and it turned into a cracking game, ebb and flow, chances at both ends. I thought I'd made it 2–0 on the night when I eased one of their defenders off the ball eighteen yards out and smacked it into the top corner, but the referee ruled it out for a foul. What, me? Well, if you want to be picky...

So we battled on, the game on a knife-edge. If they scored they would have the crucial away goal. They had this forward named Rocheteau, a bit of a George Best lookalike, and he kept wriggling free, firing in shots. We could never relax when he was on the ball. Just after half-time they got a break from midfield – it was their left-sided midfielder Bethenay on the ball, striding forward, still a fair way out – and I was tracking back, trying to get goal side and confront him or get a tackle in. Seconds before I was about to challenge him he let fly from about twenty-five yards, They talk about these new balls moving in the air but this one swerved about a yard and flew past Clem. It was the only time the Kop was quiet, but it didn't last. They were soon back in full voice and then Ray Kennedy put us 2–1 up, but we still needed to score again because of the away goal rule.

Two things happened to see us through. Bob Paisley sent on David Fairclough and, if it was possible, the Kop cranked up the volume even more. How could anyone not be lifted by such support? I know it made the hairs stand up on the back of my neck. I felt I could run through a brick wall and nothing would stop me. Davey lived up to his super-sub tag when he ran onto Ray's pass and amidst all that noise and mayhem he just stroked the ball into the corner of the net like it was a practise match. I know he doesn't like to be known as 'super sub' and always thought he should be starting games, but you have to respect the decisions Bob and the coaches made. They recognised he was the perfect impact player. Around Anfield he was known as 'The Whip'. That was because the boss would send him on in games with one instruction: to get past the full-back and 'whip one in'. So it got to the stage where the boss would turn to Joe or Ronnie and say, 'Shall we send The Whip on?' and the nickname stuck.

As I say, he was the perfect impact player. There have been a few over the years, players who could come on and turn a game but couldn't necessarily do it over ninety minutes, and I suppose that's how they saw Davey. And he can look back now on nights like that and remember it was his goal that put Liverpool into the semi-finals of the 1977 European Cup.

You would have thought in the last four of the competition we would have faced an even tougher task, but in reality our opponents FC Zürich were a pretty modest bunch. The aggregate score was 6–1, I got a couple, and that tells its own story.

That set up a meeting in the final with Borussia Mönchengladbach. They had won the Bundesliga three times on the trot and had replaced Bayern Munich as the strongest team in Germany. In their side were stars like Rainer Bonhof, Uli Stielike, Jupp Heynckes and Berti Vogts. It was a fitting finale between the best two teams in the competition. For us the added challenge was that it came just four days after the FA Cup final and, as I have already described, we arrived in Rome having seen our dreams of the treble trashed by those lucky buggers from the other end of the East Lancs Road.

All eyes were on the team sheet. What side would Bob put out? In the end he only made one change, bringing back Ian Callaghan in place of David Johnson. You can't put a price on experience and Cally had been there, more than 10 years earlier, when Liverpool lost in a titanic European Cup semi-final to Inter Milan. So it was Clem in goal, a back four of Joey Jones, Tommy Smith, Emlyn Hughes and Phil Neal; Cally, Ray and Terry Mac in the middle; Stevie Heighway and me wide, with KK on his own in the middle. It was another example of Bob's tactical awareness. Putting Kevin up front would mean that Vogts, arguably their best player, would have to occupy himself looking after KK, who was our best player, and if Kevin could pull him out of position, space would open up for the rest of us.

He was giving us the best chance he could to make Liverpool history and to win the European Cup for the first time, fulfilling Bill Shankly's ambition for the club. So we did it for Bill, for the fans and for the club, but as far as I am concerned, most of all we did it for ourselves and for each other.

The final was played at the Olympic Stadium in Rome, a big bowl of a ground, with a running track between the crowd and us. I never really liked that, it took something away from the atmosphere, but you have to hand it to the Liverpool fans, four days after Wembley there were thirty thousand of them in the ground and never a doubt about whose supporters would be making the most noise.

Liverpool fans would go to any lengths to follow us, no matter where we were playing and no matter whether a European final or a friendly. I heard a story about a fella who had been supporting Liverpool for donkey's years and he was off to Belfast, on the ferry, to see us in a pre-season game at Windsor Park. The only problem was he had just signed on after being made redundant, so he had to leave at half-time to get back to Liverpool in time to pick up his dole money.

The fans would do anything to raise the money for those trips. Liverpool's pawnshops did a roaring trade before a big European game. Clothes, pots and pans, even the family jewels, would go over the counter; scrap yards would be full of sheets of copper fans had suddenly acquired; unemployment would drop because all the blokes were doing odd jobs to get some cash. Lawns were cut, houses painted (red and white, of course).

I did the foreword to my mate Dave Kirby's brilliant book about Liverpool fans following the side across Europe when he wrote about the lad who went onto the streets with an acoustic guitar, singing 'You'll Never Walk Alone', with a sign round his neck that read 'Busking for Rome', and the fan who did a sponsored run dressed as a Roman gladiator. Part of the funds went on his trip to the European final, the rest he gave to charity.

That's why I wrote in Dave's book that standing on the pitch at the Olympic Stadium that night in 1977 was one of the proudest moments of my life. Before the kick-off we went out for a walk onto the pitch and we were totally surprised by how many fans there were. We knew how many planes were going out, but that was it. I knew the type of fella who would quite happily sell his car to be there, and they did, but we didn't think one end of the stadium would be like that when we walked out. I remember thinking back to the days when I used to catch two buses, number 86 and then the 27, to stand in the Boys' Pen and watch Peter Thompson, Ian Callaghan and Tommy Smith. Did I ever think then I would be part of such a mind-blowing occasion? As a supporter almost certainly, but as a player... don't be bloody daft!

When we saw all the red flags unfurled, all thoughts of the FA Cup disappointment went out of our minds – how could we let them down again? And when we got back into the dressing room it was Joe Fagan who quickly summed it up. 'Bloody hell,' he said, 'have you seen that lot out there?' Then Bob came in and gave us the sort of team talk I doubt any other bunch of players have ever heard before such an important game. 'The last time I was here in Rome, I was in a bloody tank liberating the place,' said Bob. 'We beat the Germans then, and you'll beat them tonight, now come on.' Any nerves we might have had vanished at that moment as everyone just fell about laughing; he was brilliant.

I've looked back at European finals around that time and there were some pretty dull matches. Forest twice won 1–0, so did we, and there was Aston Villa, Hamburg, Juventus... all single-goal results. But that 1977 final was a cracker, end to end, with loads of chances. It could have gone either way. They hit the post early doors, Clem made some smashing saves and they missed a couple of good opportunities. I remember one where Allan Simonsen headed wide when he perhaps should have scored. It all came down to who could take his chances and we were just that bit better. The opener was a beauty. Cally won the ball in midfield, on to Stevie and he spotted a brilliant run between two defenders by Terry Mac, slipped it through and Terry slotted it home. We had sliced Borussia up like a piece of bratwurst.

Then just after half-time Borussia equalised, and I have to admit, I played a part in the goal because it was my back pass to Phil Neal that was intercepted by Simonsen before he hit a beauty from the corner of the box. I would have been proud of that one. Phil blames me, but I don't know what he was doing overlapping me, because he shouldn't have been there. I had turned around and I went to give him the ball because that's where he should have been, so it was all his fault. Whatever, it threw us out of our stride for a while and they could have scored again if it hadn't been for Clem, who went down at Stielike's feet to smother his shot. A brilliant, brave save, and it turned the game.

We went up the other end and won a corner. The next few seconds have been shown time and again, burned into the memory of every Liverpool supporter. Stevie fired in the flag kick and there was Tommy Smith charging through like a bull elephant to thump his header into the top corner. What a moment for Tommy, in what was supposed to be his last-ever game for Liverpool. It was nothing less than he deserved for everything he had done for the club. I couldn't have been happier: he had been my hero, my inspiration, my mentor and my friend. When I started out in the first team, he was right behind me and I couldn't have asked for a better player to back me up. Good on you, Tommy! Still, I always kid him about that goal. I tell him he wouldn't have scored if it hadn't been for me. 'Look at the video, Tommy,' I say. 'It was me who took their player away from the post otherwise he would have headed it off the line.' Tommy comes back at me. 'You must be joking,' he says. 'No one was stopping that header!' And to be fair, there was still a defender on the line – but he never saw it.

Now it was like a home game, with those fantastic supporters filling the Rome night with their songs. They had pinched this chant from St Etienne, 'Allez Les Rouges'... I wonder what the Germans made of that? Kevin Keegan, who was bound for a European transfer after the game, fittingly had the final say. All through the match he had been on fire, running Berti Vogts ragged. And he took him on again, charging into the box, and Vogts simply couldn't get there in time. He took KK's legs and Nealy stepped up to put the penalty away. At 3–1 there was no way back for them and we finally got our hands on that enormous cup.

It was the start of the mother of all celebrations. While the fans painted the city of Rome red, back at our hotel we had this massive winners' banquet. Ray Kennedy, my brothers and me were sat in the corner. I remember we were all grabbing bottles of Bacardi and hiding them under the table; I don't know how many people were there but it was the only way we were going to get a drink. It was absolutely packed. No problems, but I kind of got the idea there was an overspill, with a load of our fans gate-crashing the evening celebrations, some of them even grabbing the cup for a souvenir photo. I couldn't see anything wrong with them getting in, it added to the whole atmosphere of the night. After all, what we had just done was for them and we couldn't have done it without them. Anyway, we got our food, there was loads of stuff to go at – and then suddenly the table resembled the carcass of a dead animal; it was like a plague of locusts had moved across the table, stripping it down to the bone.

Everyone was hitting the booze like there was no tomorrow, everyone except Bob Paisley. I remember him saying afterwards that he didn't have a drink because he wanted to remember every minute of it. I guess that tells you how special he thought it was.

We recovered in time to board the plane home but nobody had a clue what was waiting for us when we got back to Liverpool. You remember those newsreel scenes from the days when The Beatles flew into America, every space taken up by screaming fans? Well, that day we were the rock and roll stars of Liverpool. We came out of the airport and the bus had to slow down because there were so many people lining the route into the city centre. Then, as we reached the fire station on the corner by Bryant & May, all the engines were outside and they let off their sirens as we went past. That went right through me. I'm not that emotional but that did me. It's then that you realise this was what the people of the city had been waiting for and how much it meant. And the partying didn't stop there because there was still the important matter of a testimonial game for Tommy Smith – and the perfect chance to show off the trophies we had won. More than thirty-five thousand fans came out for Tommy, for what turned out to be a night to remember. The Kop was in full voice. Bobby Charlton picked a guest team for the opposition: Norman Hunter, Alex Stepney, Jack Charlton, Bobby Moore, Ian St John, Peter Thompson and Joe Royle all played. And the game finished 9–9! Clem scored a couple and so did Tommy. I'm not sure if that was what persuaded Tommy, but he decided to delay his retirement for another season and I, for one, was certainly not complaining.

Looking back, that was about as good as I could ever hope

my football life could be. Two seasons into my career as a Liverpool first team player I had two League Championships, a UEFA Cup and now a European Cup. And that win over Borussia will always rank as the pinnacle for me. We had just lost at Wembley yet we picked ourselves up to win the big one.

And I reckon this is probably a good time to put to bed a popular myth from that period. Kevin Keegan came home from Rome wearing a big pair of sunglasses, covering up a black eye. The story was that I had had a go at him for not trying his best in the FA Cup final a few days earlier because he was saving himself for the big European game. Well, as my dad once said, 'That was a rumour that was started on the Number 86 bus to Penny Lane.' It was all based on other people's perceptions of how they thought I would feel and how I would react because, top and bottom of it, Kevin didn't have a particularly good game at Wembley. But I would never have thought of Kevin not trying, and I would certainly never have dreamt of accusing him of not doing so. No, I had nothing to do with his black eye.

The truth is, it was an accident. The morning after the European Cup final some of the Press lads were milling around the hotel pool. We didn't always get on with the Press, especially the London boys, because they only ever came to see us get beat. Anyway, some of the lads grabbed hold of one of them, it might have been Jeff Powell or Steve Currie, I can't really remember, and they decided to throw him in the swimming pool and, as it was kicking off, Phil Neal's elbow came up and caught Kevin in the eye. It was as simple as that.

CHAPTER SIX

FAREWELL, KEVIN, HELLO, KENNY

We all knew Kevin Keegan was leaving Liverpool after the final and heading off to play in Europe. He had been linked with one or two big names, including Bayern Munich and Real Madrid, so it came as a bit of a surprise when he went off and joined Hamburg instead, something I have never really understood. Kevin was a big star on the international stage and he could have had his pick of clubs, so why did he choose Hamburg? To be brutally honest, they weren't that good.

We played them in the first ever European Super Cup in 1977, a two-legged tie between us, the European Cup winners, and Hamburg, who had won the European Cup Winners Cup. We drew the first match in Germany 1–1 and the return leg should have been a celebration night for the Kop and Kevin to say their farewells. But the Anfield crowd had a different agenda that night and there was a real urgency that came down from the terraces. There were mixed feelings about Kevin not putting the club first – the fans didn't like that. You can never argue with a player wanting to move on and better himself but the fans don't always see it that way and they weren't too happy with Kevin. They wanted goals and we duly obliged, hammering six past Hamburg to add another bit of silverware to the trophy room. We were on fire, but it was the crowd who really willed that result; we didn't have anything to prove to Hamburg or Kevin, we were just superior. I still don't know why he went there. If Hamburg had won 6–0 I could have understood it, but they just weren't good enough.

Still, they came up with half a million quid to take him so I guess Kevin did OK out of the deal, but it left us all back at Liverpool wondering how we would go forward without him. That was when Bob Paisley pulled off another of those inspired decisions of his when he spent the Keegan money straight away, shelling out a club record fee for the best player in Scotland, Celtic's Kenny Dalglish. They paid £450,000 for him and somebody told me recently that it works out at about £2.5m today. Imagine signing Kenny Dalglish for that sort of money. Makes you wonder what has happened to football when Spurs can pay £26m for a player like Erik Lamela, who would have struggled to get in our reserves.

Signing Kenny was a statement of intent from Liverpool that they weren't prepared to rest on their laurels, despite having had such a phenomenal season. Bob and the board, and the fans, and the players, wanted more so we were all excited by the thought of Dalglish coming in – along with another Scot, a central defender by the name of Alan Hansen. This was a signal to the rest of the First Division that Liverpool were ready to go again. It would turn out to be another successful season but, because of a bloke called Brian Clough and his Forest boys from Nottingham, it would also have its setbacks.

Who would have thought a team could come out of the Second Division and beat us to the First Division title? For the next twelve months they were like a thorn in our side, stopping us from winning the Championship, the League Cup, and then dumping on our aim of winning the European Cup three times on the bounce. We wanted Liverpool to be up there alongside Bayern Munich, Ajax, even Real Madrid, in the European record books, but Cloughie's Forest got in the way.

I suppose losing Kevin and then bringing in Kenny did upset the balance of the team for a while. As always happens, opponents had started to work our style of play so, for the 1977/78 season, Bob opted for a heavier midfield with a more fluid, pacier attacking formation, preferring David Johnson to John Toshack up front, and it took time to adjust. League results didn't go as well as we had hoped. There were five defeats before Christmas, and too many draws. We weren't dominating teams in the Liverpool way and Bob knew he had to act – so he went out and bought Graeme Souness from Middlesbrough.

Here was a player I knew from bitter experience. We had played Boro the season before, straight after the St Etienne European tie. The St Etienne game had been a bruiser against

115

a top team so come the Saturday at Anfield, we had a few guys nursing injuries and we were all, mentally, knackered. The last thing we needed was another battle, especially in the FA Cup, but that's what we got and Mr Souness was their chief warrior at that time.

We won the game 2–0 and I remember picking up a Sunday newspaper the next day to see this big picture of me lying on my back on the turf, with my hands and knees up, and Graeme has his left hand round my throat and his right hand clenched, fist drawn back, ready to punch me in the face!

It was the climax of a tough old afternoon, with plenty of tackles flying about. What happened was that Graeme had got the ball out near the touchline – my territory – and he was about to knock it up the line when I came in and got between him and the ball. He didn't like that one bit, especially when I was doing everything I could to stop him getting it back, sticking my arse into him, spreading my shoulders and lifting my arms like a pair of bat's wings. I was solid and he was trying to push me out of the way. All I could see out of the corner of my eye was Graeme looking over my shoulder to see where the ball was. It all happened so fast, but I'd had enough and, as I brought my arms up, I popped him on the nose with my elbow. It wasn't a full-blown jab, just a little 'hello' really, but as anyone will tell you, it does smart a bit.

Can't say I blame Graeme for being a bit pissed off with me and that's when he manhandled me to the floor and looked like giving me a right-hander as I'm yelling, 'Go on, punch me, and you're fucking off!' All good fun, really, and I got away with it because neither the ref nor the linesman were very close to the incident and they hadn't seen my little indiscretion. But no one held grudges. When Graeme joined Liverpool in January 1978, we just shook hands and nothing was said. Now we were on the same side and any differences had to be put behind us. Suddenly, Liverpool had a really potent force in the middle of the park. When you pooled the two strengths of his character and mine, the result was formidable. These days, Graeme and I get along famously, except when we are up against each other on the golf course.

A lot of people have asked me who I would consider to be the hardest player I ever played against. David Speedie was a fearsome player. We are the best of mates now, but we used to kick lumps out of each other, and Bryan Robson was another who would never hold back.

To be honest I was never bothered about confronting any of them, but I have to say Graeme Souness was definitely someone I preferred having with me rather than on the opposite side. For me, he was the complete central midfielder, a tremendous player and a great acquisition for the club. Liverpool have had more than their fair share of talented midfield players, but he was the most influential of all. He had the sort of presence that meant his team-mates instantly trusted him, while the opposition were instantly wary.

Still, arriving with a big reputation didn't cut the mustard at Anfield and Souness had to learn how to play within our system just like everyone else. I always remember one particular training session being run by Joe Fagan. He was working on our midfield shape with Ray Kennedy, Souness and me. We were up against five youngsters on a small pitch, being drilled to close people down. They started with the ball and it was our job to stop them progressing up the pitch, with me on the right, Souness in the middle and Ray on the left, working as a single unit, picking up the nearest player, pushing them this way and that.

We had been doing this type of work for about ten minutes when Joe marched on and ordered us to stop. Then he sent the youngsters away and took the three of us to one side and gave us an almighty bollocking. First, he had a go at Ray for not getting across to help Souness quickly enough. Then he bollocked Graeme for not backing me up, and finally, he pointed at me and said, 'Jimmy, when the ball comes over this side, you have to close him down', and I'm thinking to myself, 'Well, that's what I have been doing!'

I kept that particular thought to myself because Joe Fagan was the last person you would answer back and we just carried on with the session until he called a halt and sent us off for a cup of tea. I was still a bit peeved at being told to do something I was already doing, but as Ray and me were walking across the car park Joe comes trotting up and puts an arm round our shoulders and says, 'By the way, that telling off – that was nothing to do with you two, you were doing it the right way. It was that Souness boy who wasn't doing it right,' and that's the way Joe Fagan worked. He was fantastic.

Some people might argue, but I don't think the midfield quartet Bob put together – Case, Souness, McDermott and Kennedy – could be bettered. Even Alan Hansen said so and I have always thought he knew what he was talking about when it came to football. I don't think anyone else spotted it, but it was Bob Paisley who came up with the idea of moving Ray Kennedy to the left side of midfield. He thought Ray had lost his appetite for front running, always getting kicked from behind, and it turned out to be another masterstroke. Already he had Terry McDermott as a certain starter, I had come through to take a place on the right side, and now he had Souness to take over from Ian Callaghan, to my mind the greatest servant Liverpool has ever had.

Graeme was the final piece of the jigsaw. He brought fierce tackling and ball winning skill, tremendous vision and the ability to make the killer pass. It was the perfect combination of talents. We were there to win the battles first and then play football and we didn't lose many battles. We could all dig in, although it is generally Graeme, Terry and me who are remembered for being, how should I put it? First to the ball? But let me tell you, Ray Kennedy was no slouch when it came to putting a foot in – and he was bigger than the rest of us. We never set out to be aggressive, despite what some people might think. That was only if they were taking advantage of other players on the pitch. Well, you look after your own, don't you?

That season we never got the consistency in the League that people usually associated with Liverpool and after we lost two games in a row, which was unheard of at the time, there was a headline on the back page of the *Daily Mirror* on a story written by Chris James, massive letters covering the whole page, which screamed: 'The Empire Is Crumbling'. Bob Paisley didn't like that sort of thing and so he called a Tuesday team meeting, which was also unusual because normally we would only have a meeting on a Friday to talk about the next day's opposition. So we went into the training room and there was Bob with Joe on one shoulder and Ronnie on the other, and we looked at each other and wondered what the hell was going on.

Bob said, 'Right, we've lost two games in a row', and he held up the newspaper cutting that said 'The Empire Is Crumbling'. 'We've been looking at youse all in training and we've been watching what you've been eating, trying to find out what's been going bloody wrong. Well, we have found out what's been going wrong, haven't we, Joe, Ronnie?' There was a pause, and then Bob continued, 'Some of ya have been playing GOLF,' and then he said, 'Our training schedule can cope with all your beer and your women... but the bloody golf is out!' and with that, all the coaches stormed out of the room.

League results might not have been so good that season, but Europe was a different matter. It was my favourite hunting ground and if you look at my Liverpool goal scoring record, thirteen goals from twenty-three European games, compared with twenty-three from a hundred and seventy League appearances, you can see how comfortable I was with the continental style of play.

That season I scored four times, two against Dynamo Dresden, a goal against fading Benfica in their less-than-impressive Stadium of Light, and one in the semi-final against our old foes, Borussia Mönchengladbach. That put us through to our second successive final, at Wembley, against FC Bruges, but I cannot say my memories of that game are particularly pleasant. We went into it without Tommy Smith. Somehow the old bugger had got himself injured by dropping an axe on his foot while doing a spot of DIY! That let in Alan Hansen, who had begun to work his way out of the reserves.

Before the final, I was relishing the prospect. Two years earlier I had scored one of the goals that had helped Liverpool beat Bruges in the final of the UEFA Cup so they held no fears for me, especially at Wembley, which made it almost a home game. But unlike Rome and the thriller against Borussia, this was a tight, tetchy affair. Bruges seemed happy to hold their lines and try to deny us scoring opportunities, but they didn't seem too bothered about trying to score themselves. It was almost as if they were afraid of what we could do rather than trying to win the game themselves. A couple of times we went close – I had a free kick their keeper did well to save – but they certainly upset our rhythm and it was no surprise when Bob Paisley decided, just after half-time, that he had to shake things up. I just wish it hadn't been me who got the hook.

The game needed a spark, something different to break up the predictable pattern of play, so the boss sent on Steve Heighway and handed me a tracksuit top to keep warm. At the time I was gutted – no matter how obviously tactical a substitution is, you always feel as if you've done something wrong as a player. But I suppose Steve was, well, quicker than me. Anyway, you can't argue with any of Bob's decisions and this was another one that turned out alright. Stevie had only been on the pitch two minutes when Graeme Souness came up with a peach of a through ball for Kenny Dalglish and he just dinked it over the keeper, cool as you like. The goal was pure Dalglish and proof indeed, if ever it was needed, of what a great player he was; certainly the best I ever played with.

I could name plenty of other talented players from my days at Liverpool, Brighton and Southampton. Lads like Matt Le Tissier, Alan Shearer and Kevin Keegan, of course. When Kevin left Liverpool I thought the whole world had fallen apart.

But Kenny came in, pulled on Kevin's number seven shirt while it was still warm and made Liverpool an even better team. Kevin was great, but a completely different player. Just say we were attacking the Kop end, I was playing wide right and I would slip a pass inside to Kevin and dart down the line, waiting for a return pass inside the full-back. Kevin would turn the other way, run across the pitch with the ball, beat two or three and then turn and come all the way back, beat the same two or three players and then pass it to me.

Kenny was different. He would get the ball, look across the pitch towards Steve Heighway on the left and at the same time clip a reverse pass with his left foot without looking, just inside and beyond the full-back, where, in his mind, I should be – oh, and by the way, that is precisely where I was... such vision and awareness.

Kevin was all about pace and power, bags of energy, but Kenny had artistry and awareness. One of the best pieces of skill on the football field I have ever seen, and I was fortunate to witness it from close quarters as I was only a few yards away on the same Anfield pitch, was a goal scored by Kenny. It went like this: I was wide right, hugging the touchline, and Kenny was more central. Alan Hansen was on the ball in our own half as we were kicking towards the Kop when, all of a sudden, Kenny makes a run from the middle of the pitch towards the corner of the eighteen-yard box and Hansen obliged with a perfectly weighted ball to that spot. Most forwards would take the ball towards the corner flag with their centre back close behind, but not Kenny. As the ball landed, he chopped it back behind him with the outside of his right boot. Now the ball was settled just on the edge of the eighteen-yard box on the right, with the opposing centre back trying to put the anchors on. Kenny turned and with the inside of his left foot, curled the ball round the keeper and into the far top corner of the goal. I was amazed at what I had just seen and could do no more than put my hands together with the rest of the supporters. So when Dalglish scored that sweet goal at Wembley to win the European Cup for the second successive season, it just confirmed my opinion of him.

That victory was the cue for another tour of the city centre. God, I loved it. That was when you saw the unique spirit of the Liverpool fans and you could feel the special bond that exists between them and the players. We finished that 1977/78 season with another European Cup, and for me there was a personal moment of pride when I was voted European Young Player of the Year. It was the year that an Italian magazine called *Guerin Sportivo* had organised the very first European awards event and I had to go over to Italy for the ceremony, flying into Bologna and staying for a few days in Ravenna, on the Adriatic coast.

Paolo Rossi won the main prize and then presented the Young Player of the Year trophy. Antonio Cabrini of Juventus came third, the Dutch lad Johnny Rep was second, and I got the nod for the award. For me just to be mentioned in the same company as players like that was a big deal so to be given the European Young Player of the Year trophy was all a bit surreal, really. Since then it has been won by players like Marco van Basten, Paolo Maldini, Roberto Baggio and a bloke named Ryan Giggs, who played for some other club.

Yet despite getting that award on the back of winning the European Cup, I look back and think we could have won the League that season, and we should have won the League Cup but somehow lost them both to Brian Clough's Forest.

It took until Christmas before anyone started to take Clough's team seriously, but we had seen enough to know they were a decent side. We couldn't beat them in the League, drawing home and away, more often than not because of the sheer brilliance of Forest's keeper, Peter Shilton. I didn't know it at the time, but our paths would cross again, years later on the south coast at Southampton.

But for the League Cup final Shilton was missing and we had enough chances to win it by a country mile but they all slipped away, even one that fell nicely for Kenny Dalglish. Perhaps we should have known then that it was not meant to be. For the most part, Forest parked the bus and held out for a 0–0 draw and a replay the following Wednesday at Old Trafford. And that was the night we got stuffed by referee Pat Partridge.

There was nothing between the teams again but Forest got a break through the middle – I think it was John O'Hare. As he ran clear with only Clem to beat, Tommo clipped his ankles right on the edge of the box. As professional fouls go, it was a good one, even though it would have got him sent off today. Tommo had to take him out and we all reckoned there was about a foot to spare, but Partridge decided it was inside the area and John Robertson scored the penalty.

Then Partridge did us again. Terry Mac scored what looked like a perfectly good equaliser but Partridge decided he had handled it and gave Forest a free kick. If you can find some TV footage it's plain to see the referee got both decisions wrong, but that's how it goes sometimes: fair play to Forest. Apparently that was the first time a club had won the Division One title and the League Cup in the same season, so it wasn't a bad double for a so-called 'little' club.

What we didn't expect was getting knocked out of the European Cup a few months later by that same 'little' club. It was just the luck of the draw that saw us playing Forest in the first round and there's no disguising the fact that we blew it, big time. The first leg was away at the City Ground and to be honest, we forgot it was a European tie and went gung-ho for the win. I think we had just played them so often in a short spell, we were too used to each other. All the games rolled into one and then a result popped up. It was a shame it was in Europe and that we got drawn against them so early on. It's hard to explain in words what we did but it wasn't the usual 'close the gates, play a cagey game' type of away performance that had served us so well in Europe.

Those were the orders that came from the bench but to be honest, they were things you automatically did, away from home in Europe. Keep the ball, take it to the corners, work it up the field, and if you go a goal down don't respond to the bait of trying to get the goal back too quickly because that's how easy it is to concede a second... and that's just what happened against Forest. I think maybe it didn't feel like a European tie and so we didn't mentally treat it as one.

Of course, Forest went on to win the Cup but I wasn't that interested. I have to say, I was pretty gutted, I think we all were, because we wanted to be the ones to put Liverpool's name on the trophy for the third time in a row. But once we were out, it was gone from my mind.

You have to hand it to Cloughie, though. To take a club like Forest to two successive finals puts him up there among the best managers – just not so good as Shanks or Bob Paisley. We quickly came to recognise they were a good side and looked forward to those games because they were always a challenge. Run through the team and you have to admit they were good from front to back: Shilts, Larry Lloyd, Kenny Burns, Martin O'Neill, Ian Bowyer. I remember he used to roll down the top of his shorts to make himself look hard. He wasn't the one that bothered me, though – for me the main man was John Robertson.

He was like Matt Le Tissier; not a lot of pace but he could drop a shoulder and leave you for dead, and if you gave him enough room, he could whip in a cross for Garry Birtles or Tony Woodcock before you could close him down. I remember meeting him and I was quite surprised to see him with a fag in his mouth, but he was like that when he played. So casual and laidback, he was almost horizontal.

Clough got the best out of them and you cannot argue with their record around that time: they seemed to be at Wembley almost as many times as we did. But one thing is certain, it could never happen today. I can't see how a Championship side could do what Forest did – win promotion, then the title, then the European Cup not just once but twice. They would need to win promotion with a team of Premier League quality and then move on from there. Today it is virtually a case of buying trophies and if it doesn't happen straight away, the manager gets sacked.

I do like watching the football today, but it's all about the top four or bust and that's not right; it doesn't enhance the League. When you think that Manchester United had to shell out £37m for Juan Mata, just to keep them ticking over, what chance is there for clubs like Stoke, Hull or even Southampton, who have done well to bring their own players through? The very best they can hope for is to try to get into the Europa Cup and for my money, that's a non-event.

Back in my day, every team had a chance because they all had their stars. Keith Weller and Frank Worthington were at Leicester, Roger Davies at Derby, Alan Hudson at Stoke, Rodney Marsh and Stan Bowles at QPR. And the only time you got to see them play was on *Match of the Day*. That sort of player has gone and if a club does produce someone outstanding he is quickly snapped up by one of the top four or, like Gareth Bale, tempted by one of the big guns in Spain. The game has lost a lot of its artistry and what there is has to be imported from South America, Spain, even Belgium. I suppose, for younger fans, it is what they have grown up with and they don't know about the standard of football in my day. I know the money is there now, but I'm still glad I played when I did.

As for Cloughie: would I have liked to play for him? I don't see why not. I would play for anyone. My attitude was if you do your job, you will be OK. But there was another side to Cloughie and I'm not sure it would have worked out. From what I've read, he liked to boss his players about, tell them what to do and make them toe the line. That's all right up to a point but he sometimes said and did things that were out of order. Didn't he once punch Roy Keane? I wouldn't have been able to go along with that. I would have told him what I thought and I reckon that would have soon led to a parting of the ways.

I remember once lining up in the corridor before a game against Forest, he kicked me on the back of the leg. Right out of the blue, he just came up behind me and gave me a little kick and said something like, 'Hello, young man.' I just turned round, looked straight back at him and said, 'That won't do you any fucking good!'

I also remember someone at Liverpool piping up about Clough letting the Forest players have a drink of wine with their pre-match meal but when we suggested it, we were told in no uncertain terms it was never going to happen at Anfield, so forget it.

Forest chased us all the way that season but we were back and won the League by 8 points, with a little help from a certain national newspaper that these days is never mentioned around the city but back then was the working man's bible. Not long ago I was up in Liverpool and wandering round a well-known supermarket when someone grabbed a big handful of copies of that particular newspaper, about ten in all, and threw them in with the toilet rolls. Scousers don't forget.

But back in the seventies it was the newspaper everyone read, especially footie fans, and they put up a prize of £50,000 – that's right, £50,000, which would be a cool quarter of a million now – for any team who managed to score eighty-four League goals during the season. Remember, in those days there were forty-two games so to average two goals a game was some target.

We didn't start to think about that until we got into April and then suddenly the realisation sank in that we could actually win the cash. At the end of April we got a 0–0 draw at Forest, which left us with five games to play, still needing a dozen goals to reach the 84 mark. We were shooting for the First Division title, but there's no doubt the added incentive of that fifty grand provided an extra bit of motivation.

How else would you explain this sequence of results? Bolton away, 4–1, Southampton at home, 2–0, Aston Villa at home, 3–0, Middlesbrough away, 1–0. The Boro game had been a tight affair and with only David Johnson's goal to show for it, we were still two short and the final match was away at Leeds United. Going to Elland Road was never easy. Already we had clinched the title but there was still the little matter of that prize riding on the result.

No one needed reminding of what was at stake. When David Johnson put us ahead after twenty minutes or so, it was within touching distance. One more goal and we would be in the money – and it fell to me to hit the golden goal. I don't remember much about how I scored – it could have gone in off my backside for all I cared. I ran towards the Liverpool section of fans who were well aware of what was happening and I gave them a Max Bygraves' 'You Need Hands' type of gesture, just to let them know we had won the cash and to say thanks for their support.

That wasn't quite the end of it, though. The newspaper had to pay up but then came the question of whether it would be taxed when the pot was shared among all the players. As it turned out, the money was put into a special account and then one player took the case to a tribunal to argue that it should be deemed a bet and therefore tax-free. There was only one player capable of taking on that particular job: young, smart-arse Steve Heighway, with all his grammar school qualifications. Of course he won and we all got a decent share of that newspaper's generosity. Nice one, Stevie!

It looked like we were on for a League and Cup double until we let ourselves down in the semi-final against Man U. We'd beaten them 3–0 at Old Trafford in the League, and 2–0 at Anfield, but we just didn't perform in that cup tie and lost after a replay, at Goodison Park of all places. There was also a 4–3 aggregate defeat in the European Super Cup final against Anderlecht, which all added up to another season of mixed fortunes.

But winning the League again meant we could have another crack at the European Cup and we set our sights on getting through to the 1980 final, but just as we had done twelve months earlier at Forest, we went out at the first hurdle after a trip to Russia that I will never forget.

We had to play one of Russia's top sides at the time, Dinamo Tbilisi. What a nightmare that turned out to be. We were OK at Anfield, but we let an away goal slip. David Johnson gave us the lead, they equalised and then I got another European goal for the win. But we knew that away goal could be decisive and it would be far from easy in Russia. Well, just winning the game would have been tough enough, but trying to do so while the Russians pulled every dirty trick in the book just made it all the more difficult.

It started at the airport in Moscow when we landed. As soon as the customs people found out who we were they did everything they could to hold us up. We were there for hours being told to go to this desk and that. They even ordered the kit man to take everything out of the kit baskets for no good reason. Then we had to catch another plane to go to the very south of Russia, to Tbilisi in Georgia. When we got outside the terminal it was freezing, about minus five degrees F. All David Fairclough had on was a V-necked sweater and he was desperately trying to find someone to lend him a jacket.

We eventually arrived in Tbilisi and discovered a town about as attractive as the inside of a prison door. The hotel was a grey, dismal building in an ugly square. We were so knackered and all we wanted was a good night's sleep. Fat chance! Here we were, behind the Iron Curtain, in a country that didn't allow public demonstrations and what happened? At 2.30am we were woken by the most almighty racket coming from outside. I looked out the window and there were Russian fans chanting and carrying flaming torches. No chance of sleeping through that lot.

It got worse when we arrived at the stadium, with over ninety thousand of their fans creating one of the most hostile environments I can remember. We lost 3–0, I got substituted and all in all, I was well and truly pissed off. It couldn't get any worse, could it? Well, as a matter of fact it did. After all that, the first thing I wanted was a bevy back at the hotel with a few friends who had made the trip and who turned up with some Bacardi and whisky. Just what the doctor ordered. But first we had to go to a reception, listening to a lot of speeches in Russian, translated by an interpreter – not that any of us were listening.

They brought out some food, which looked decidedly unappetising. I remember Terry McDermott pointing to a pile of caviar and warning us, 'Lads, stay clear of that black jam, it tastes like fucking fish!' The only promising gesture was an endless supply of champagne. Trouble was, on top of an empty stomach, it was a recipe for disaster so by the time we had escaped to the bar and ordered the beers, I was a little the worse for wear and in a foul mood. We'd lost to Forest on the previous Saturday, then travelled to a godforsaken corner of the world, got stuffed 3–0 and to cap it all, I'd been substituted. I was steaming. So when I walked into the room to join my friends, the first thing I saw was all the Press lads sitting around drinking whisky, laughing and joking without a care in the world. I blew my top because I knew, inwardly, that the London Press only travelled with us to see us get beat and to see them knocking back the booze and sitting there smug as Cheshire cats, I saw a Jimmy Case shade of red.

With one sweep of my arm I knocked all their drinks off the table and then I pointed to each one of them and said, 'Jeff Powell, I hate you; Steve Curry, I hate you; John Keith, you're alright; Colin Wood, you're alright, and Chris James, I hate you.'

At that moment Ray Kennedy stepped in and saved me from further embarrassment when he grabbed me by the neck and marched me outside. 'You can't do that,' he told me, 'it'll be all over the papers tomorrow. Get back in there and apologise.'

It stuck in my craw, but I knew he was right. I went to the bar and bought a round of drinks to replace the ones I'd knocked over, put them on a tray and took them back to the table. Then I placed a drink in front of each individual and proceeded to explain my actions. I told them things had built up inside me over the past couple of weeks and the defeat that night, and being substituted, had tipped me over the edge. I apologised and then finished my little speech by looking at them all and shouting, 'And if you don't believe me, I will punch your fucking lights out!' – at which point Ray gave me a friendly tap on the chin and led me out of the bar.

Left: From left to right: my sister Linda, me, brothers Frank and David, and my mum on a trip to the seaside in Rhyl, North Wales.

Right: Springwood County Primary U10s school team: we won the local schools' cup. The one with the ball is John Gidman who went on to play for Everton, Man Utd, Man City, Aston Villa and England. I'm the one standing behind him and as you can see I was small for my age.

Left: Another school photo, this time Toxteth High School U15s. I have the ball this time and the boy behind with his hand over my head is Paul Cliff. At that time I thought he was a better player than me, but he went into the music business instead.

Above: My Sunday League team, The Blue Union. This was before the kick off of the National Cup final held at Holly Park, South Liverpool's ground. The picture captures our captain Tosh Jones introducing our team to the local dignitaries and I'm in the middle.

Below: Here's the team photo taken just before kick off at Holly Park. The full name for the team is The Blue Union and Stevedores Dockers Social Club.

Left: I look pretty happy at scoring against West Brom at Anfield.

Right: Auditioning for the Chippendales? Emlyn Hughes, left, Ray Kennedy and myself – a stupid picture for a tabloid paper that we got talked into doing.

Left: When I hammered in this equalising goal in the 1977 FA Cup final I thought we would go on and win it, but unfortunately we lost the game 2–1 to – and I hate saying it – Manchester United.

Top: Borussia Monchengladbach were a great side with players like Rainier Bonhof – who is marking me here on a Liverpool corner and had won the World Cup with West Germany at the age of twenty-two – but I always thought if we stuck to our own game we would come through and win.

© *Peter Robinson/EMPICS Sport*

Centre left: I got my hands on the European Cup as we did a lap of honour around the Olympic Stadium after a cracking 3–1 win over Borussia Monchengladbach in the 1977 final.

Right: There's no better feeling than this. Local boy made good… I raise the European Cup aloft in Rome, what a night.

Above: Bob Paisley's all-conquering Liverpool squad. I'm second row, third from the left, standing directly behind my hero Tommy Smith. That collection of trophies came in my first full season in the first team.

Below: We took an open-topped bus from the now-John Lennon airport to the city centre. Thousands upon thousands lined the streets all the way as we brought the European Cup back to Merseyside.

Top left: This was a semi-final match at Highbury for Brighton against Sheffield Wednesday, and this strike was the first goal in the game, and one of the best goals I have ever scored. I was well pleased with that one.

Top right: This I how I played football: the ball at my feet, eyes searching for the right pass.

Below: A Charity Shield match against West Ham United and two hard men came together. I'm up against the tough West Ham captain Billy Bonds.   © *EMPICS/PA Images*

Above: Brighton's FA Cup team from 1983 – my last chance to add an FA Cup winners medal to my collection.

Centre right: Even after the 1983 FA Cup final replay when the Seagulls lost 4-0 to Manchester United the supporters were brilliant and we went over and gave them a wave to show what they meant to us.

Left: In the blue of Brighton – I think I became something of a fan favourite on the south coast, also playing for Southampton and Bournemouth.

Above: Another FA Cup semi-final goal, this time against Everton at Maine Road. My Liverpool heaven, I'm getting the congratulations from Terry McDermott and, to the left, Kenny Dalglish. Another golden goal.   © *Popperfoto/Getty Images*

Below: My collection of medals laid out on my mum's table (not bad for a lad from Allerton!).

CHAPTER SEVEN

TIME TO MOVE ON

I didn't know it until the last possible moment, but as we moved into the 1980s my time at Liverpool was running out. Perhaps I should have spotted the clues. Incidents like the one in Tbilisi must have been noted by Bob and the coaches and I have to confess, it wasn't an isolated occasion. There was something of a drinking culture at Liverpool in those days. Ray and me were usually at the heart of it, along with Terry McDermott, Phil Thompson, Emlyn and Smithy – everyone, really.

If we went out for a night in Liverpool, there were so many people wanting to buy us a drink you could easily have ten pints lined up in front of you and not pay for any of them. It never really got out of hand, but there was the time when I was breathalysed and I suppose that didn't go down so well either.

That was in 1979. I had some friends over from Manchester for the weekend and we had a few beers, as you do, when we decided to get a takeaway… and I volunteered to fetch the food. It was only just up the road, I still had my slippers on in the car, but I got stopped and that was that. I have no excuse, I shouldn't have done it. At the time, I never really thought that it might affect my place at Liverpool.

The coaches knew all about the drinking – it went on at all the clubs – and my thinking was that because we trained all week, played a hard game on a Saturday, to go out and have a few drinks afterwards was something we had earned. In my view, we were just letting our hair down a bit, but the club in those days didn't like that type of thing. I suppose they must have thought I was a bit of a bad lad.

After I left the club attitudes changed and certainly after Bob Paisley and Joe Fagan had left there would be incidents of players getting into a few scrapes, and still they were kept on at the club. One player terrorised half the Wirral, with about four police cars chasing him, but the club kept him on. Let's put it this way, I'm not the only number 8 in the history of Liverpool FC who has been arrested, but my punishment was to be eased out of the club. It doesn't seem to happen these days.

We never did the drinking at the wrong times and we never let it interfere with our performances on the field – not counting the time we took on a bunch of Alicante waiters. The game was played on 29 May 1975 at the Estadio Municipal F; we won 2–1.

We had gone on an end-of-season trip to Benidorm and it

was bedlam. To justify the trip, it was agreed we would play this team of waiters and let's just say when it was time to kick-off, one or two of us were feeling the effects of over-indulgence. Terry Mac was suffering from a banging head-ache. He went to control a pass and missed the ball completely; his vision had gone. Somehow I managed to score a goal with a header at the far post... but I nearly butted the goal post at the same time!

Then there was the time after a derby game with Everton, they took us up to Blackpool and we checked into the Imperial Hotel. There were drinks on the house, a bottle of wine in the restaurant, all the usual stuff. After the meal we went into the lounge, Ray and me were sitting together as always, then there was Kevin Keegan at another table, playing cards, Phil Thomson heading off to the disco, when Joe Fagan came through the door. He wandered round the tables, chatting to the lads, and when he got to Ray and me he said, 'See Kevin over there, and Phil... I know what they will be doing tonight, but I haven't got a bloody clue what you two are going to get up to.' As he walked off, Ray and me just nodded to each other. It was a kind of unspoken warning.

Not everyone enjoyed a drink. There was one time, coming back from the Charity Shield final in 1977, and I noticed that Kenny Dalglish, who hadn't been with the club long – in fact, I think that was his debut – wasn't joining in so I asked him to have a drink.

'I don't drink, Jimmy,' he said.

'You *must* drink,' I insisted.

'No, Jimmy, honestly, I don't,' he told me.

I shook my head and turned to one of the lads and quietly remarked, 'Well, he won't make it.' How wrong could I be?

I suppose the final nail in the coffin of my Liverpool career was when Ray and me were arrested in a hotel in North Wales for fighting. We were taken to court in Llangollen and admitted assaulting the hotel owner and his son, but I have to tell you what actually happened was a bit different to what the prosecution told the court.

Basically, they maintained we had attacked the two men without provocation but they didn't pay any attention to what had led to the incident. Well, as they say, there are two sides to every argument... and this is the gospel according to Jimmy Case. We had just beaten Everton and the club took us away for a mid-season break, a sort of bonding trip, if you like, and we ended up at this fantastic country hotel in Llangollen called the Bryn Howell. We all went off to our rooms, me sharing with Ray, as we always did, and then into the bar. It was a good atmosphere, especially as we had just beaten the blue lot. We went into the restaurant, had a nice à la carte meal, a decent bottle of wine, not the usual Blue Nun or Black Tower, a bit to drink on the club's tab as long as we didn't go too far, and then Terry McDermott came across, pulled up a chair and ordered his à la carte meal... a pint of lager and a beef sandwich!

The only downside was that the hotel was a bit quiet and there was only one pub within walking distance, about a mile away, so Terry told us some of the lads were getting the hotel minibus for a trip into Chester. I said to Terry, 'Give us a shout when you're ready and we'll come with you,' and then Ray and me carried on with our meal. We finished up and went into the bar and sat with Joe Fagan and Roy Evans, waiting for Terry to fetch us. At that point Albert Lloyd, who owned the hotel, came in so we asked him what time the minibus would be taking the lads into Chester.

'Oh, they went about half an hour ago,' says Albert. We weren't best pleased to be left twiddling our thumbs in the middle of nowhere while the lads were out on the town, but we ordered another bottle of wine and settled down for a quiet night. Then Albert offered to take us to another hotel not too far away, called The Chain Bridge. He drove us down there and it was a bit more lively than his place because they had a disco on that night, so we stayed there for a couple of drinks and Albert had a couple with us, then he brought us back to his hotel.

By this time it was residents-only in the hotel bar and Ray and me were the only ones left in there – as usual. We were chatting to the barman when Ray got up to go to the main reception, which was along a corridor. Funny, but I remember it had these nice wooden panelled walls. Anyway, he just wanted to use the telephone – remember, this was before mobile phones – so I was left with my pint, sitting by the log fire in the bar area.

At that point Terry Mac walked into the hotel, Ray spotted him and grabbed him by the scruff of the neck. 'Why didn't you come and get me and Jimmy?' he asked. Terry never had time to answer. From behind Ray, the hotel owner Albert grabbed his arm, thinking he was going to hit Terry, and said, 'Come on, Alan.' Ray wasn't best pleased to be called Alan and pushed his arm out to shrug Albert off and must have caught him. In a split second Albert had chinned Ray square on the jaw and they started scuffling, just as Albert's son John came in and decided to get involved.

By now someone had telephoned the police and all this was kicking off while I was still sitting in the bar, minding my own business. Then someone ran in and told me Ray was fighting in the foyer. When I got there he was holding his face, which had started to swell up, and I said, 'What's up, mate?'

'Albert just chinned me, and then his son started having a go,' said Ray.

'Well, if it's like that,' I said, 'let's go and sort 'em out,' and as it all kicked off again, in came the police, storming through the door, and they slapped the handcuffs on Ray and me. As we were being led away, I spotted Terry Mac sneaking upstairs, trying to hide behind the wallpaper. The last thing I saw was David Johnson leaning out of his bedroom window as we were put in the panda car, shouting, 'Don't worry, Jimbo, I'll get Joe and Ronnie.'

They stuck Ray and me in separate cells and we had to cool our heels while the coaches sorted it out and eventually we gave our statements and were bailed.

When it came to the court case, we followed the club's legal advice and pleaded guilty to assault but the nonsense that came from the prosecution made it sound a lot worse, stuff about throwing chairs and kicking people, which never happened: guilty by fabrication. The truth was, Albert struck the first blow, but we were fined £150.

Our lawyer told the court it was all because of the tension and pressure of the derby game earlier in the day, playing in front of a crowd of fifty-five thousand, adrenalin pumping, and then we had come away to relax and, as he put it, 'perhaps both of the accused drank far more than they were accustomed to.'

Well, I don't know about that. I was accustomed to drinking a fair bit when I set my mind to it. What it was, Ray was in trouble, I was his mate and I went to help him out. That's how it was with us. There's something he said later that I'll never forget. Ray said: 'Fines, court appearances, jail... we were bad for each other. We had a bit of fun, but we did it at the right time. At hotels, when we asked for the room key, the receptionist would dive under the desk and say, "Not you two again!"'

Ray and me were kind of thrown together in the first place, not long after I got into the first team. To start with, I was rooming with Joey Jones. I suppose they paired us because we were the youngest. I can't remember where we were, but Joey wasn't on the particular trip and Ronnie Moran asked if I would share with Ray. It was not a problem, I was happy to share a room on trips with any of the lads.

The more I thought about it, no offence to Joey who is a great lad and a great mate, but I realised I could learn a lot more from a professional point of view from a player like Ray. He had won the double at Arsenal, where he had had that great partnership with John Radford, and I thought his experience could help me in my career. That's how it started, but it soon went much deeper than that. We just fitted together so well; we're both easy-going, plus we were both very tidy. Our room was always immaculate and anyone who has travelled with footballers will know that is not always the case; usually they leave their rooms looking like a rat's nest. You know, we even polished each other's shoes. If Ray was watching TV, I would pick up his shoes and give them a shine, and vice versa.

Back in those days, you had to pay for all your extras so we used to take our own sandwiches to have a snack in the room. My mum would get this lovely ham off the bone from John Lewis's in Liverpool. Of course, as soon as the lads caught on they would come knocking. I remember Cally and Alec Lindsay were both a bit partial to Mum's ham sarnies.

Ray and me became inseparable, like Morecambe & Wise. If I came through a door he would be one step behind me. We were always there for each other and everyone knew it. Tommy Smith came up to me one time in some hotel. Ray was in the next room and Tom said: 'Can you go and sort your mate out. He's arguing again and you're the only one he will listen to.'

That's why we are best mates to this day. And we took that relationship out onto the pitch and I knew he would never let me down. He could be a moody bugger, a bit grumpy at times, and he could over-react to situations. As I said, I am pretty easy-going and there would be times when I couldn't understand why he was getting so worked up. I used to say to him, 'What's wrong, mate? Calm down, it's not worth it.' What no one knew at the time was it had nothing do with Ray's personality: it was the first sign that physically, something wasn't right.

We both left Liverpool at about the same time. I went to Brighton in 1981 and Ray went off to Swansea the next year. John Toshack was the manager down there and Swansea had been making headlines by climbing up from the Fourth Division to the top flight. But, just as quick, it all started to unwind, and they were relegated the following season. Ray and Tosh fell out. Tosh didn't think Ray was trying in games, but what he and Ray didn't know was Ray was showing the first signs of Parkinson's Disease. That was the end of Ray's career and the next thing I heard, he was off to hospital for a series of tests. They sent him to the Royal Middlesex in Goodge Street, close to London's West End, and when I went up there with him, that's when all the details came out. It was a big shock, I can tell you.

Here was this hugely talented footballer, someone who looked as strong as an ox, facing up to the prospect of a future as a virtual invalid. The doctors put him on medication and he is still on it to this day. He went back to the northeast to live so I don't see him as much as I used to, perhaps two or three times a year. He came down to Liverpool one time to see a game and people who knew him back in the day didn't recognise him, but he is OK and he has never lost his sense of humour. We were up in his bungalow one day, watching football – it was when Kevin was up at Newcastle. I said, 'Kevin's doing OK,' and Ray just said, 'Aye, but he's won nowt!' Then Ray asked me if I wanted a cup of tea, I said, 'Yes', and then made a joke about him shaking because of the Parkinson's by adding, 'but I will make it this time. I want my tea in the cup, not spilt in the saucer like last time.' He laughed at that one.

So off I went into the kitchen to make us a cup of tea and about a minute later I heard a thud on the floor in the hallway. I looked over to the doorway and all I could see was Ray's head just at the bottom of the door, looking up at me. I just stood there and said, 'What the fuck are you doing down there?' and he said, 'Oh, I stumbled.' We were both laughing our heads off as I helped him up.

When I went to leave, just outside the front door someone had left a bag, collecting for old clothes. I said to Ray, 'There's a bag here, it says it's for any old clothes,' and quick as you like Ray said, 'Tell them I don't want any,' and we started laughing again.

It's sad to see him like that, and it's very hard, walking out of his front door and leaving him, but Ray seems to be OK in himself. He copes with the illness, but I do know he has his dark days. The PFA did, at one time, help fund a wet room for him so he could take a shower while sitting down; also the former players at Liverpool sorted out a new, sturdier kitchen for him because he was forever breaking the drawers by leaning on them as he was getting about. And he has his son and daughter, Dale and Cara, living nearby, so Ray's OK.

We've got a lot of great memories to share – the games we played, the scrapes we got into. It might have been the reason I had to leave Liverpool, or one of them, but I tell you what, I wouldn't swap a minute of those times I had with Ray.

So I had begun to get the feeling that my time at Liverpool was coming to an end through the 1980/81 season. We didn't have a brilliant time, by our standards, in the League – we ended up finishing fifth – then we were knocked out of the FA Cup by Everton. There was another League Cup success and we got through to another European final, but my place was coming under threat from a bright young lad named Sammy Lee. Sammy and me are good mates, but he didn't bother me at the time. I was more than prepared to give him a run for his money, but he was about twenty, I was nearer twenty-eight, and I suppose Bob and the boot room boys could see a ready-made replacement for me. And one who didn't carry quite so much baggage around.

During that season, Bob took me to one side and told me John Toshack had been on the phone pestering him for permission to talk to me about a move to Swansea. Because I knew John, I said OK. I couldn't see any harm in talking to him, but no disrespect to Swansea and Wales, it wasn't for me. At the time, I thought it was a bit strange, the way it came about, but I put it to the back of my mind and carried on as normal.

I didn't think I had had that bad a season: forty appearances out of sixty-three, League Cup winners medal, Charity Shield and on the winning side in the European Cup final against Real Madrid. Mind you, I didn't start that game, Sammy Lee did, and I only got on for the last four minutes. But it was another trophy for Liverpool, thanks to Alan Kennedy's goal. I know I wasn't on the pitch at the time, but I had to mention Alan's goal because I wouldn't hear the last of it if I didn't. I mean, he just goes on and on about it!

We had a real laugh after the game, the usual good celebration. I remember sitting outside our hotel on the Champs Elysées, with the European Cup sitting proudly on the table, when Ray Clemence suddenly chirped up, 'It wasn't as good as the first time in Rome, was it?'

Everyone just stared at him in amazement and I turned and said, 'What the hell are you on about? We've just won the European Cup for the third time!'

'Oh, not that,' said Clem. 'I meant the bloody party after the game!' We fell about, but what I didn't realise was that for me, it would be the last laugh at Liverpool.

We had another major trophy to celebrate and another Beatles' style homecoming with the cup, riding the open-topped bus through Liverpool, the fans clinging onto lamp-posts, hanging off tree branches, anything to get a glimpse of the team and that trophy.

That summer there was a lot of newspaper talk about Howard Kendall wanting to take me to Everton. I would never have gone there anyway, but all talk of a transfer across Stanley Park was stopped at boardroom level. I remember someone telling me the comment among the directors was, 'If Jimmy Case went to Everton, it would cause havoc'.

I was ready for the next season and reported back to Melwood to start training. Then we went off for three build-up games in Switzerland. We beat Zurich 3–0, then lost to Servette, 2–1. I played in that game and in the second half I twisted my ankle and was substituted for Howard Gale. The next day my ankle was up like a balloon so there was no chance I could play in the final match, which means a friendly game against Servette of Switzerland is down in the record books as my last ever game for Liverpool, even though I didn't see that coming.

We were due to fly back to the UK the next day and that was when Bob Paisley took me to one side again and told me Brighton and Hove Albion had been on, asking about my availability. That was the second time it had happened and I don't believe in coincidences, I realised then I didn't figure in Bob's plans so I agreed to talk to Brighton. What I didn't know was that I was actually the make-weight in the deal to take Mark Lawrenson to Liverpool: Brighton hadn't asked about me, I had been offered to them. I didn't want to leave, I had never asked to leave, but it quickly became clear that something was happening.

But that's football and I don't hold any grudges. Bob Paisley thought he needed Lawrenson to improve the team and that he could do better with Sammy instead of me. Fair enough, that was his opinion and he was the boss, so who was I to argue? I would have stopped at Liverpool if I could have done and I know that if I had stayed, I could have done the job Sammy did. And I know that if I'd still been there, he wouldn't have needed to bring Steve McMahon in because I could have done his job just as well, if not better.

Without a doubt in my mind they made a mistake in letting me go. After Brighton, I played six seasons in central midfield for Southampton, hardly missed a game, and in one of the seasons the *Daily Star* rated me the top midfield player in the country. OK, I know it's only a newspaper, but it gives you an idea of how I was playing and why, in my opinion, I could still have done a job for Liverpool until I was thirty-two or thirty-three. They lost five years of me when I was at my best. But it was not to be and my view was, if they think they can do without me so be it... see ya later!

Don't misunderstand me, I wasn't bitter then, and I'm not bitter now. I accepted it as part and parcel of the game and got on with the next chapter in my life. I'm not the sort to dwell on things like that; what will be, will be. In fact, I had been more disappointed when I was turned down by Liverpool schoolboys all those years ago, and then by Burnley when I was sixteen, because at that time I thought I might never get the chance to be a professional footballer, so I will be forever grateful to Liverpool for giving me the opportunity to make all my dreams come true and for providing me with memories I will cherish for the rest of my life.

But there would be a lot more football to come for Jimmy Case after Anfield, another fourteen years of playing competitively before I was forced to call it a day, and for the most part, I enjoyed all the games, all the clubs, wherever football took me. But nothing could ever replace Liverpool. They had been in my blood from as far back as I could remember.

I missed the friends I had made, particularly Ray Kennedy, my soulmate. And I missed the people who had given me my chance, especially Bob Paisley. I have played for a lot of managers, some good, others not so good, one or two downright crap, but without a doubt Bob was the best. He was an old-fashioned boss who ran the club his way and didn't much care what anyone else thought.

Some of the statements he would come out with were priceless. I wish I could remember them all, but here are a few of the best examples: Every year the lads would have a Christmas party and it was always the captain's job to approach the boss and ask him when, or on what day, we could organise the event. That way the staff could give us a particularly hard training session on the morning before the party and then give us the next day off. But Bob hated Christmas parties and I just happened to be standing close by when Tommy Smith put the question to him.

'Hey, boss, when can we have our Christmas party?' to which came the reply, 'Bloody 'ell, Christmas bloody party! Why don't you have it in the bloody summer?'

As I have said, Bob Paisley was very proud of his war service with the Desert Rats and he would often drop in a bit of military jargon. The first time I heard it was when he was asked by one of the senior players if we could have a luxury coach with card tables and individual lights over the seats, 'like the one Arsenal have got'.

'Luxury... luxury?' replied Bob. 'I was a Desert Rat, ye know, in a bloody tank in the bloody desert. No luxury there, son,' and with that he turned round and walked off. We knew that was the end of that particular subject.

I loved his one-liners, like the half-time team talk when he said to Stevie Heighway, 'Why don't you fling the far-flung one?', meaning get some deep crosses into the box; or he asked me, 'When was the last time you drifted a one, eh?' I didn't understand at first but then realised he was asking why I hadn't got any long-range shots in.

His pre-match team talks were legendary. Every Friday we would have a team meeting before we went out to train and we would generally talk about the team we were playing the next day. Well, we had been on a winning run of a good few games and all the lads were sat down in the room, waiting for the team talk. In walks Bob, with the coaches, Ronnie and Joe, and he looked around the room at everyone and then said, 'Right, lads we've got Tottenham tomorrow, errrrrrrrr... same again,' and they all walked out. Priceless.

But even more than Bob, and the lads, I missed the fans.

Nothing can compare to playing in front of a full house at Anfield, especially one of those tense European ties under floodlights. The Kop could inspire players to achieve things they would normally not have attempted. And I like to think I had a special relationship with them. Just chanting my name was enough to raise goose bumps, but imagine what it was like to run onto the pitch, look across to the Paddock, where I had once stood to watch games, and see a banner that read 'Jimmy Case – Thunder Boots'.

There is no humour like Scouse humour and I remember playing at Anfield, on the right as usual, and there was a bit of a hold-up in the game while a player was getting treatment. So, I'm standing on the touchline, ball under my arm, waiting to take the throw-in, when a bloke sitting a couple of rows back behind me, shouts, 'Alright, Jimmy!' I looked around and with a cheeky grin, I said, 'Alright, lad.' He was munching on this big meat and potato pie and the next thing he says, 'Do you wanna bite?'

I said, 'Go 'ed then,' and I took a big bite out of his pie, much to the amazement of the rest of the crowd, who loved it. That's Scouse humour for you. Of course, they wouldn't allow it now.

I went back to Anfield with Brighton and then Southampton and, as you have read, I scored the goal in 1983 to knock Liverpool out of the FA Cup, but the fans never turned on me. At heart I was still one of them and they knew that. A few years ago, they voted me at number forty-five in a poll to find the top hundred players that shook the Kop. I will always appreciate that.

CHAPTER EIGHT

A BRIGHTON BOY

To say leaving Liverpool was a bit of wrench is the understatement of the century. And who would have thought I would end up on the south coast, two hundred miles away from my hometown, at a club like Brighton and Hove Albion?

I don't mean that with any disrespect, I'm simply stating a fact that Brighton could never be regarded as a club on the same level as Liverpool, yet they had picked up a multi-European cup winner in the prime of his life. Why Brighton? I have been asked this so many times, especially as there were one or two clubs, including Everton and West Ham, that you might describe as 'more glamorous' sniffing around. But as I have explained, the issue was largely taken out of my hands. Liverpool wanted Mark Lawrenson, Bob Paisley wanted to move on the bad boy Jimmy Case, and Brighton made me a decent offer. And just to put the record straight for the benefit of Brighton fans, I can honestly say I never regretted the move. Sure, I would rather have stayed at Liverpool and fought Sammy Lee for my place, but nevertheless, I enjoyed every minute of my time at Brighton.

I read about players today who say they will only join a club if they can be guaranteed European football, or a club that will pay them the outrageous wages they think they deserve, but that sort of thing didn't bother me. I just wanted to play football and as long as it was competitive and was my type of game and not that long ball tactic that was creeping in at the time, it didn't matter where I hung my hat, the enjoyment would be there.

And if I'd gone to a Midlands club, or Manchester or Leeds, likely as not I would still have lived in Liverpool and that would have meant commuting every day by motorway. Being behind the wheel of a car for long periods is the easiest way to pull muscles. My thinking was that if I had to move, then the further away from Liverpool I got, the better it would be. So, in August 1981 I signed a five-year contract with Brighton manager Mike Bailey and on 28 August I made my debut in a 1–1 draw at West Ham. It was the start of a four-year roller-coaster ride, during which events off the field would often overshadow what was happening out there on the pitch.

It was certainly a far cry from Liverpool and Anfield. In many ways the old Goldstone Ground was a bit of a ramshackle place; ugly fencing between the fans and the pitch, and crowds of about eighteen thousand were nothing like I'd been used to. And at first, it wasn't exactly my style of play. I can understand the way Mike Bailey was thinking: he was a good coach, with the tough job of keeping a relatively small club like Brighton in the top division, so he opted for a safety first approach. It was working as far as results were concerned, but football fans are the same the world over; they want to be entertained and they weren't all that impressed with Mike's tactics. And as any manager will tell you, once you've lost the backing of the fans, there is only ever going to be one outcome.

Collectively, there is no doubt that the players I had left behind at Liverpool were more skilful and the team was much stronger, so it would have been easy for me to go to Brighton and start lording it, banging on about all the medals I'd won and that type of thing, but I am one of those people who accepts what is in front of him and it would never have been in my make-up to go there with that sort of attitude. To be honest, I didn't find it any great problem to adjust to life after Liverpool, even though it had been my home for the first twenty-eight years of my life, the last eight spent playing for the club. There aren't many players who have left Anfield and gone on to have the sort of career I had, but I think me being a midfielder helped. It didn't matter which club I was playing for, my primary job was simple: to win the ball. Now for a striker it can be harder because they would no longer be playing with the quality of player that Liverpool possessed so they might still be making the same runs, getting into the right positions, but suddenly the ball was no longer coming through at the right moment, with the right pace, and in time that begins to affect your own performance.

And it wasn't as if I was joining a bunch of no-hopers.

Brighton had a decent squad of players, which, if you were to put it together today, would certainly be worth a bob or two. There were a lot of strong characters in that Brighton dressing room when I arrived: Stevie Foster, Sammy Nelson, Tony Grealish, Don Shanks, Micky Thomas, Michael Robinson, Gordon Smith, Andy Ritchie, Gerry Ryan; strong characters and good players.

I suppose, for me at least, that first season at the Goldstone was memorable for the two League games against Liverpool. Saturday, 17 October 1981 will always be a red letter day in my life because it was the first time I went out to play against my old club. There I was, wearing the blue shirt of Brighton, and when I got my first touch of the ball I passed it straight to Kenny Dalglish!

That game was a thriller, it finished 3–3, and I scored with a thumping header past Bruce Grobbelaar. What a strange feeling that was. I didn't really know how to celebrate so I just raised my arms and that was it. I didn't feel any great pleasure beyond it being an important goal for my team. There were no thoughts about how Bob Paisley might have felt. I don't suppose he gave it a minute, he had made the decision to let me go and as far as I was concerned, that was in the past. I was just pleased to have helped Brighton to a valuable point against the League champions.

When we went up to Liverpool for the return fixture the Kop gave me a great reception with a chorus of: 'Oh, Jimmy-Jimmy, Jimmy-Jimmy, Jimmy-Jimmy, JIMMY CASE', and I gave the Kop my one-arm raised salute, exactly how I did it when I played there. That was a great moment for me. They knew where my heart would always be... and then I helped Brighton to a 1–0 win.

Those two games were the high spots of a pretty good first season. Brighton finished in thirteenth place in the First Division, the highest position in their history. I played thirty-three times, I enjoyed my football and quickly settled down on the south coast, where I discovered there really was life outside of Liverpool, although I did have to conquer the problem of my Scouse accent.

Let's just say, when I first moved down to Brighton, I had a bit of a communication problem with the locals. I was speaking too fast for them to understand what the heck I was saying, so I had to make a conscious effort to slow down.

The move also opened my eyes to different cultures. I had never been in an Indian or Italian restaurant before I moved down there. My idea of a night out in Liverpool would be a couple of pints – well, more than a couple, to be totally accurate – and then it would always be a Chinese meal at the Golden Park on Allerton Road, washed down with a bottle of those old favourites, Blue Nun or Black Tower. If we fancied pushing the boat out, we might even run to a bottle of Mateus Rosé. But I think it's fair to say that the inhabitants of Brighton and Hove were just a little more sophisticated than in the Allerton of the 1970s and I was introduced to the many and varied attractions of decent food and fine wine. It was an education I really appreciated.

It would certainly provide a welcome distraction from the football, which began to go sour in my second season at the Goldstone. In the League we played good football, but we couldn't get the results; I think we played too open a style and kept getting caught out at the back. By Christmas we had only won five or six times and perhaps inevitably, Mike Bailey got the sack.

The man to take over was the chief scout, Jimmy Melia, who had been an Anfield favourite back in the late 1950s and early 60s. At that time, with morale pretty low, Jimmy was the ideal man to come in and lift everyone's spirits. He was a real character was Jimmy, flamboyant in his John Travolta white suit, a real extrovert, and while he might not have been the greatest tactician the game has ever known, he definitely lifted the players and set us up for that amazing FA Cup run.

I know he had an effect on me. My form so far that season had for some reason been patchy. I'd always prided myself on my consistency allied to a strong work ethic, but until Jimmy took over, I had been missing that vital spark. Jimmy tapped into my thoughts and from then on, certainly in the Cup games, I hit something near my peak. But as good as we were in the FA Cup, Jimmy couldn't weave his magic week in, week out. He lifted the players for those big cup-ties against Newcastle United, Manchester City and especially Liverpool, and led them to the brink of the biggest achievement in their history. But on a day-to-day basis he couldn't find the right blend, the necessary impetus to lift us up the table.

We were a young side and concentration was a problem. It was OK for the big games, especially in the Cup. We were always on our toes for those games and as Cup fever began to grip the town ahead of every tie, I was back in the eye of a storm I recognised so well. The fans were everywhere, offering encouragement, wishing us good luck. Just like back in Liverpool, it reminded me that at the end of the day it was the supporters you were playing for and we all wanted to make it happen for them. But we couldn't do it week in, week out. The Cup run was brilliant, the fans turned out in their thousands, everyone was lifted by the magic and the dream of Wembley, but against that background, it was difficult to get the team motivated for the never-ending struggle for League points. Too often in run-of-the-mill games, against teams we really should have beaten, we were let down by individual mistakes and they mounted up and cost us in the end.

We might have won through to Wembley, to give me another shot at a winners' medal – the nearest I would come, as it happens – but finishing bottom of the First Division wasn't in my plans. But if you were to ask any Brighton fan if they could turn the clock back and swap that day at Wembley for Division One survival, I don't think many would take up the offer. It provided them with a special memory that will always be there, while a dozen League games are soon forgotten. If only players today would realise that the FA Cup was that important and, as far as I am concerned, it still is.

Despite relegation, I never gave a thought to moving on, just to stay in the First Division. Having signed a five-year contract to play for Brighton, the longest of my career, I was determined to do everything I could to help them get promotion. But just as it is now, the old Second Division was a tough league to get out of. There were some big clubs down there, like Chelsea, Newcastle and Leeds, and every game was a scrap. Don't get me wrong, I relished the challenge but a lot of the football was long ball stuff and that didn't suit me. I wanted to get the ball down in midfield, but too often it went flying over my head.

As fate would have it, there was another high spot in a season in which we finished a disappointing ninth in the League. We were drawn to play Liverpool again in the FA Cup, and again the tie was at Anfield. Sadly, I had to watch from the bench this time because I was suspended, but it was a great day for Brighton as we beat the Reds 2–0 to set up a fifth-round tie against Watford, who, back in those days, rode the crest of that Graham Taylor/Elton John wave in the First Division.

Now, remember me telling you about the old guy Henry, who was the odd job man at Anfield? Well, in those days every club, no matter what level they played at, had one of those guys who did all the running around, all the little tasks, unseen for most of the time, but absolutely necessary to keep the club ticking over. Brighton was no different. His name was Jock Riddle and he stood about five feet nothing in his cotton socks and wore glasses with thick lenses that looked like the bottom of a bottle.

What a character! It was one of his jobs to wash all the match day and training kit in a small building next to the main stand. There wasn't much room to manoeuvre around four huge washing machines, but it was a cosy corner and one day I wandered in there for a chat and we got talking about previous jobs he'd had. I nearly fell on the floor laughing when he said that at one time he used to train elephants in a circus. So when we turned up at Watford for the FA Cup tie Jock had already laid our kit out and then, as usual, he had sloped off for a crafty smoke. It's an unwritten rule that in the last hour before a game, while the lads are getting changed and listening to last-minute instructions, no one is supposed to enter the dressing room. Well, I was up the top end of the changing room, getting stripped next to Steve Foster and Steve Gatting, and about fifteen minutes into our routine, the door was flung open and at the top of his voice Jock shouted, 'Hey, Fozzie, someone here wants a word with ya. It's a little fat fella, he said his name was Elton!' That, of course, was Elton John, who was standing right behind Jock and heard the lot. We were all in stitches and I have to say, I can't remember a better incident to release the tension before a big game.

Winning at Liverpool was an even bigger shock than the previous season, certainly a greater achievement. In 1982 we were both rivals in Division One and, on its day, our squad at that time was more than capable of giving even the best sides a run for their money. But this time around one or two Brighton players had moved on after relegation, including Michael Robinson, who had gone in the opposite direction with a transfer to Liverpool, and he was in their team that day.

There are all sorts of memories of that day, not least how strange it was to see Joe Fagan in charge of the Liverpool team, having taken over from Bob Paisley. And you have to remember that Brighton stopped Joe's team from winning all four trophies that season. They took the First Division title, won the League Cup and finished off by winning the European Cup for the fourth time. But we stopped them making history and setting a record that might never have been broken.

All these years later, I am still not sure how it happened.

Perhaps Liverpool wanted it too much, having been knocked out by Brighton the year before. They were nervy and disjointed from the kick-off and when we scored twice in a minute – the goals came from Gerry Ryan and Terry Connor – it threw them completely out of their stride. But everyone in a blue shirt played above himself that day. Somehow we managed to keep Ian Rush and old boy Michael Robinson quiet and in goal we had a giant of a keeper named Joe Corrigan, who stopped everything that was thrown at him.

If we are talking about characters, then Joe is right up there. Not only was he a damned good goalkeeper, he was also great to have around the dressing room, always game for a laugh, and we soon became good mates. Just picture this scene: It was Brighton's Christmas party and we were off to an Italian restaurant on Church Road in Hove called Toppolino's, which had been booked exclusively for the players. As always, it was a compulsory fancy-dress affair and the idea was all the lads would keep their outfits a secret until we turned up at the restaurant. But Joe came round to my house to get changed and my first glimpse of him was when he walked into my living room and there he stood, all 6 feet 5 inches of him, dressed in a fairy godmother outfit complete with white tights, tutu-style dress and with his ugly sister make-up on, struggling to zip up the dress. 'Zip me up, Jimmy,' says big Joe, and so there I am, struggling to pull the zip of a fairy dress over the great hairy back of a giant footballer. I just wish someone had had a camera.

The restaurant was booked for lunchtime after a hard morning on the training field. It would be an even harder afternoon's drinking and then the plan was to head into the Lanes area of Brighton in the evening for a few more beers. Needless to say, we were all on foot, with no one driving. Walking through the middle of town, we came to a set of traffic lights and Joe decided it would be a good move to direct the traffic so we could all get across. Remember, this is Joe Corrigan, dressed in a ballet dancer's dress, who was standing in the middle of the road, beckoning cars facing a red light to go, and stopping cars that were on the green light. To this day I am still not sure how he survived that incident without having his collar felt.

Joe is a big, soft lad with a heart of gold, but he has a painful way of showing it. One of his party pieces is to catch you off-guard with a short jab, either in your ribs or on the side of your arm, to give you a dead arm. He doesn't mean to hurt you, he just doesn't know his own strength, and one day he gave our physio, Mike Yaxley, one of these playful punches... and broke two of his ribs!

That was Joe, a star performer on the pitch and a bloody clown off it. He was one of the heroes that day as Liverpool battered Brighton in the final quarter of an hour, but they couldn't get the ball past him and it ended 2–0 to the Seagulls in front of a stunned and silent Anfield crowd. For the second season in a row we had knocked out the favourites for the Cup. I could see us going all the way to the final again.

I know our next opponents, Watford, were a division higher than us but I really fancied our chances of going to Vicarage Road and getting a result. There were no great stars in the Watford side to frighten us... well, they did have a lad called

John Barnes but the only thing I can remember about him that day was the penalty he gave away. Danny Wilson scored for us from the spot, but by then we were 2–0 down after some fairly average defending and when they got a third in the second half, the dream was over.

Those weren't happy times for Brighton. There were financial problems off the field, trouble on the terraces. Then there was a game when Chelsea came down and their fans rioted. It was a tough ask against that background for the new manager Chris Catlin to build a side that could win promotion. The team that had got to the cup final a couple of years earlier had been more or less broken up: Gary Stevens had gone to Spurs, Steve Foster to Aston Villa, Tony Grealish to West Brom. I wasn't looking to follow them, but then Chris Catlin took me to one side and told me Southampton's manager, Lawrie McMenemy, wanted to have a word with me about a move along the coast. I drove over to Southampton with the understanding that if the talks went well, I would sign that afternoon. For me it was an easy decision: I would be going back into the top division. The money was not a great issue but I was happy with what he offered and so all that was left was the medical, which I passed, even though I had a slight groin strain at the time. At 4pm that Tuesday afternoon I put pen to paper and was straight in the team that Saturday to play Spurs at White Hart Lane. I remember early on I caught Gary Lineker with a strong challenge and I immediately thought, 'Yes, I'm back.' And one look at Lineker's face was enough to tell me I had won my first battle... he wouldn't be straying back into midfield any time soon.

I've heard all sorts of things about the transfer over the years. Lawrie said he brought me in as a stop-gap until the end of the season after Steve Williams went to Arsenal, me being thirty-one at the time, but I was still playing first team football at The Dell long after Lawrie had left. And I heard from a Brighton director that Chris Catlin had told the board my legs had gone. Whatever the reason, I made the switch for £30,000 and played for six seasons at Southampton, hardly missing a match. Altogether I played over two hundred times, more than I played for Liverpool. So much for those legs!

Another comment was that McMenemy, who left for Sunderland not long after he signed me, wanted someone who wouldn't be overawed by a dressing room that already had characters like Joe Jordan, Mick Mills and Peter Shilton in there. Well, reputations have never meant that much to me and before long Joe Jordan and me had become big pals. People think he was a bit of an animal – probably think the same about me, to be fair – but Joe was one of the good guys. We became very good pals and that hasn't changed to this day. When I first arrived, I was in digs in a Southampton hotel and sometimes after training, Joe would ask me what I was doing and I would say I was just going back to my hotel. Joe would say, 'No you're not, you are coming to my house for a meal', and he would serve up a lovely pasta dish, just the job.

Now Shilts could be just the opposite. He had a fantastic career and we had faced each other many times, especially when he was playing for Forest and we were both going for all the silverware. He had already been at Southampton a couple of years when I arrived in March 1985 and at first he seemed friendly enough but one night, about halfway through the following season, we were up in the players' lounge, having a few beers at the start of what turned into a bit of a twenty-four-hour session, and my opinion of him changed.

First stop was a wine bar called Simon's, where we stayed until closing time, and then I suggested the lads came back to my hotel. There was Glenn Cockerill, Shilts and myself, and we stayed in the bar until the early hours. Usual thing, I was the last man standing. Shilts was a bit the worse for wear, having been on the brandy, so I told him to get his head down in my room. Next morning, after breakfast, he invited me down to his local, a pub called The Clump in Chilworth, for the proverbial hair of the dog.

As we settled down over a pint, in walked Gerry Forrest. Now, Gerry was a talented full-back, who had been signed from Rotherham United and he was a good lad, always up for a bit of banter in the dressing room. He decided to join us as we headed off to another pub called The Malt House on the Romsey to Stockbridge road. This was Sunday lunchtime, back in the days when pubs closed at 2pm but Shilts said we could get a drink after hours. I went outside to wait for the taxi and as I walked back into the pub to fetch the lads, I saw Shilts pushing Gerry away. I guessed they were just messing about, so at the time, I didn't give it much thought.

But at the next pub Shilts began holding court at the bar to anyone who would listen to his stories. I pulled Gerry to one side and asked what had gone on earlier. Apparently, just as the taxi arrived, Shilts was taking a last swig of his beer and it went down the wrong way. He coughed it up and spat it back into his glass so Gerry said, just joking, 'You had better leave that, Shilts, you're struggling a bit.'

Shilts didn't like that one bit. 'I never struggle,' he said, 'and anyway, you're only a Second Division player!'

I was livid. Next time I got to the bar all I could hear was Shilton telling his crowd, 'When I'm England manager ...' Shilts was being a bit of an arse so I challenged him to meet me before training the next morning to sort it out, man-to-man. He didn't turn up.

Nothing more was said and we got on OK after that, but I haven't got Shilts on my Christmas card list and judging by the fact that I never receive one from him, I guess the feeling is mutual. You can't knock his statistics, though. He played more than a thousand games, still pulling on his boots at the age of forty-eight, and he won a hundred and twenty-five caps for England. It could have been a lot more if the England manager, Ron Greenwood, had been able to make up his mind which keeper was the better: Shilts or my old Liverpool team-mate, Ray Clemence. Personally, I would give Clem the edge. They were both great keepers, both great shot stoppers, but Clem was more likely to come out to get the ball, helping to take the pressure off the defence, while Shilts liked to stay on his line. Clem was a better sweeper behind the defence as well and was always prepared to come out of the area and clatter a forward with his knees.

When Terry McDermott and me were playing in midfield for Liverpool we were always happy to let an opponent take a shot from twenty-five yards because it rarely got past Clem from that distance. If they got any closer, one of us would move in with a challenge. I suppose for me the bottom line was that Ray Clemence was a team player while I always thought Shilts was more aloof.

There is no doubt that moving to Southampton helped me to keep playing at the top level for so many years. I played central midfield and my forward line was Matt Le Tissier on one side, Alan Shearer in the middle and either of the Wallace boys on the other wing, Rodney or Danny. They were like whippets. With those young lads in front of me, my forte of winning the ball and passing it to the flair players was made a lot easier.

Alan Shearer was knocking on the door when I first moved to Southampton and I watched him grow from an eighteen-year-old boy to a twenty-four-year-old man. It was interesting to see him develop. Technically, there were more gifted players than him at the club. I remember particularly a lad called Leroy Whale, but for some reason it didn't happen for him and he drifted off to non-league football. Alan made it happen: he had natural power, pace and could finish, and he never stopped working to make himself a better player. He would stay behind for hours after training, just shooting from any angle, working at his craft.

I played in his debut when we beat Arsenal at The Dell and he scored a hat-trick and you didn't need to be a football genius to realise how good he was. There were some games when he couldn't do anything right, but he never stopped working, never passed up the chance to get into a scoring position. I respected that. And once he came out of a barren spell the goals would start flowing again. He had the sort of attitude a lot of today's players would do well to copy.

You couldn't say that about Matt Le Tissier, though. Now there was a player with an exceptional amount of natural ability, the sort of player Southampton fans, or anyone else for that matter, would pay good money to watch. He arrived at The Dell in May 1985 at a time when the reserve team was bursting with young talent and just watching the games, it was pretty obvious one or two would soon be in the first team but Matt was the one player who really stood out.

Certain people used to say he displayed a distinct lack of commitment, that his stamina was lacking, that he wasn't as fit as he could be. That might be why he only played eight times for England. Eight caps? For a player who possessed that amount of natural ability, it was ridiculous. The trouble was that England managers didn't know how to get the best out of him. But here was a player who could do things few could match. Matt could produce a piece of skill to turn a game on its head, conjure up a goal out of absolutely nothing. He won eight caps more than me but everyone knows he should have had a lot more.

I think Glenn Hoddle made a big mistake when he left Matt out of his World Cup squad in 1998. It must have been a big disappointment – no one knows better than me how it feels to be passed over by an England manager – but to his credit, I don't think it affected Matt that much, certainly he never showed it, because he was the main man at Southampton for many more seasons, just proving how wrong Hoddle was. Matt was a flair player and in his day, one of the best in the game, yet Hoddle, of all people, couldn't recognise the value in taking someone like him to the World Cup.

Admittedly, he could frustrate the hell out of you, but that came with the package. There was a testimonial game at The Dell in 1997 for another good mate, Francis Benali. I was in midfield, with Graeme Souness; Matt was playing up front. Inevitably, the ball would find its way to Matt's feet and he was determined to put on a show, so he tried to dribble past every defender he could see. The trouble was, when he lost the ball, Souey and I had to sprint back to defend while Matt trotted behind us without a care in the world. After it had happened a few times, Souey shouted across to me, 'I don't know how the fuck you played with him!' Thing was, Graeme was the manager of Southampton at the time.

There was one time when I tried to bring him into line. I forget who we were playing, but Matt was in one of his moods, loitering on the right wing and not really getting involved, and I turned to my midfield partner, Glenn Cockerill, and said, 'Look at Matt out there, he doesn't look too interested today. When we win the next ball, give it to me and watch what happens.'

Sure enough, Glenn popped the ball to me and I passed it to Matt on the right wing. He just tapped it straight back. At this point I looked across to the left, where one of the Wallace boys was waiting as if I was going to knock a long ball cross-field. Then I suddenly turned back and passed to Matt instead. He had got the full-back zeroing in on him so he just gave it back to me again, expecting me to look elsewhere, but I thought sod him. This time, instead of rolling it back to his feet, I fired it chest-high, just as the full-back was ready to fly in with a tackle. So what did Matt do? He chested the ball down, flipped it over the defender's head, looked up and crossed it onto Alan Shearer's head and he scored.

The thing about Matt was that he loved a challenge. Some of the basic things were just too easy for him. He could waltz past defenders two or three at a time – without any great pace. With the ball at his feet, bearing down on goal, he would try the impossible and usually succeed, a wayward spirit but a genius of a player.

Mind you, his memory is not always what it should be. In his biography he suggests that I owed him £200 he had won off me at cards. Sorry, Matt, but you should know I never played cards. I was too busy cooking and serving up the meals and drinks for all the players on the trips back to Southampton.

CHAPTER NINE

SUPER
SAINTS

I don't have any regrets about my life in football. I stand by the decisions I made, the clubs I chose to play for. Those decisions kept me playing for more than twenty years, so why should I look back and wonder what if? But that's not to say there weren't disappointments. They go hand in hand with any footballer's career: you cannot win every match, take every chance, or make every tackle.

In my mind, there are three major disappointments from a career that covered the best part of seven hundred competitive games, the majority played at or near the top level of English football. The biggest disappointment would be that I never won the FA Cup, despite playing in two Wembley finals. I would also count never being selected to play for England at full international level – I thought I was good enough but others disagreed. As for the third... in my six years playing more than two hundred games for Southampton FC, we never won a trophy.

They were great years when I was playing at my peak, surrounded by as talented a bunch of players as any manager could collect at that time. We had a wonderful blend of youth and experience. I've told you about the young lads like Shearer, Le Tissier and the Wallaces, but the seam of talent that passed through The Dell during my time there went a lot deeper. We had Shilts in goal, for a start, and that meant we were always in with a chance against any opposition. When he moved on Tim Flowers took over and became another top keeper. Then there were the regulars, like Mick Mills, Mark Wright, Neil Ruddock, Kevin Bond, Nicky Holmes, Micky Adams, Mark Dennis, Barry Horne, Francis Benali, Gerry Forrest, Russell Osman, Andy Townsend and Glenn Cockerill. We were a match for anyone in our day and we came so close, so many times.

During those six years at The Dell we got to two Cup semi-finals, losing to Liverpool in the FA Cup and Football League Cup; we more than held our own in the old First Division, played in Europe, and under two great managers, Lawrie McMenemy and Chris Nicholl; we were a breath of fresh air, scoring goals for fun. But at the end of the day, there is nothing to show in the honours column. We entertained the fans and we gave them moments to cherish and remember, but the bottom line is that we came away empty-handed.

Lawrie had signed me from Brighton for £30,000. I was thirty-one and the transfer was seen by many as a stop-gap deal for he put me on a one-year contract. But I never asked for anything more, I was never given anything longer, and that was fine by me. I would let my football do the talking and if they could find someone better, fair enough.

Clever guy was Lawrie, he had a knack of persuading big names who were perhaps just past their best to give life on the south coast a try. He brought Alan Ball to Southampton ten years after he had won the World Cup and that started a trend that he repeated over and over. Star players who had been at the big clubs, like Peter Osgood of Chelsea, Ted MacDougall (Manchester United), Charlie George (Arsenal), England captain Mick Mills from Ipswich, Shilts from Forest, and of course the transfer that shook everyone up came when he persuaded Kevin Keegan to come back to England after his less-than-stellar time at Hamburg.

Like that other fella I played for from the northeast, Bob Paisley, ex-Guardsman Lawrie was also very shrewd. He had never played at any decent level of football and he knew it was no good him trying to tell players like Keegan, Charlie George, Joe Jordan, Mick Channon and the like how to do their jobs. Instead he surrounded himself with the best players he could buy, created the right atmosphere for them to flourish and then let them get on with it. He would open up team meetings with a few words and then let the senior players take over; he picked the team but allowed the older players to play to their strengths. His greatest asset in my eyes was that he got good players to play for him and that really is the secret to any team's success.

McMenemy left not long after I joined Southampton. I played the last ten games for him until the end of the season before he went off to join Sunderland. Ex-Saints defender Chris Nicholl took over and he carried on the good work. I got on well with Chris. I was getting older by then, I was thirty-one, maybe thirty-two, and there were some who were expecting me to slow down, to be there just when needed. I suppose it's understandable that they didn't see me as someone who would play virtually every game, season after season. But I saw it differently and so did Chris. In fact, I will never forget the day he called me into his office and made me captain. Smart move that, and I was made up. I was determined never to let him down nor give him an excuse to say, 'Well, Jimmy, I think your time is up.'

At the end of each season most club managers ask their captains into the office for a chat about the team and last season's performance, etc. And I always asked him: 'Are you going to buy another midfielder? If you do, I will see him off as well.' But there were also a couple of occasions when I said to Chris that if we were to go on and do something meaningful and actually win something, we would need at least two more players of a certain quality.

And when it came to renewing my contract, I would go into his office armed with the programme from the last game of the previous season, which had all the appearances printed in it. 'Look here,' I pointed to the list. 'I've missed two games... and that was when Robbie James fell on me! If that doesn't warrant a new contract then I don't know what does.' Chris never said anything, he would just slide a piece of paper across his desk and when I looked, it had my basic salary figure, plus bonuses, written down. That was good enough for me: no arguments, no negotiations, I signed on for another year.

That's not to say we always saw eye to eye. Chris was a real student of the game and he was one of the first to latch on to the notion that diet was important, especially what you ate before a match. I had always been a steak man, but Chris had read somewhere that pasta was the ideal preparation. I remember the first time he took us to a local Italian restaurant before a big game and ordered pasta for everyone. I told him I wanted a fillet steak same as usual. 'Steak is no good for you,' said Chris. 'It takes eighteen hours to digest and it affects the blood flow to various muscles.' I just looked at him and then reminded him of all the medals I had won at Liverpool, eating steak before a match. Enough said, I got my steak!

And it was the same with training. I've always kept myself fit, but I preferred to work with the ball. One day, Chris brought along this England international sprinter, can't remember his name, to try to build up our speed off the mark. He had us running hundred metre sprints: focus on a point at the end of the track, start low, pump your arms, point your fingers. 'Hey,' I said. 'I'm 34. It's a bit late to try to get an extra yard of pace out of me!'

And that's the trouble with the game today. They are trying to turn out athletes at the expense of flair; the emphasis is on fitness and I think coaches should concentrate on ability.

Here's some examples: Matt Le Tissier – he was never the fittest of players, but he was a genius on the ball; Lionel Messi – he doesn't look like a footballer, he looks overweight, doesn't work that hard, but he is the best in the world; Jimmy

Greaves – back in the day, his work ethic was non-existent but, put him in front of goal, and he rarely missed. He was a fantastic player. Fans want to see skill, tricks and great goals, not robots who just do what the manager tells them to do. Sadly, that is what is wrong with England, but I will talk more about that later.

Back to Southampton and, as I was saying, my one disappointment was that I couldn't help Chris put some silverware on the table. The fans who packed into The Dell and created a really intense atmosphere on big game days certainly deserved it, and so did the players. We gave them something to shout about and we entertained them, most of the time, but we couldn't quite break out of the middle-of-the-table pack. We were never quite consistent enough to get among the boys at the top of the League, although we were good enough, on our day, to give any of them a hiding. In 1986 we got through to the semi-final of the League Cup, I think it was known as the Littlewoods Cup that year, and on the way we came up against Manchester United in a replay at The Dell. It was possibly my best game in a Saints' shirt and one I look back on with great satisfaction... but then again, I always remember the wins over that lot.

What made it so special was this was the game that changed history. Ron Atkinson was the United manager, in the middle of a tough run of results, and the vultures were circling. The Press was piling on the pressure and there was one reporter's article I remember that said Big Ron had the look of 'a man who had just discovered a mouse in his pork pie', and we weren't about to make it any easier for him.

United had thumped us 5–1 in the League at Old Trafford, not many weeks before, and we wanted to put the record straight when we brought them back to The Dell for that League Cup replay.

Talking about Ron Atkinson, I found out from Chris Nicholl that when I was bought from Brighton for £30,000, Ron had tried to get me up to Old Trafford with a bid of £60,000; it was when Remi Moses got injured, but Southampton wanted to keep me and I never knew a thing at the time. To be honest, I don't think I could ever have seen myself playing in that particular red shirt.

The game finished 4–1 and we could easily have scored eight. George Lawrence, an unpredictable, raw-boned centre forward who scored brilliant goals but could just as easily fall over the ball, got the first with a pile-driver right out of the Jimmy Case handbook. Danny Wallace got the second and then this gangly young lad named Le Tissier finished it off. When he coolly lobbed the United keeper, Chris Turner, it was his first goal for the club and an announcement that a major new talent was emerging. Typically, Matt then did it again, with his head, to complete the scoring, but it wasn't his first goals that made history that day. That defeat got Ron Atkinson the sack and, soon after, Manchester United hired a bloke called Ferguson to replace him.

It wasn't long after that when we played United in the League, a 1–1 draw at The Dell and one of Fergie's first games in charge. Apart from one memorable incident, it was a nothing game. The match had barely been going a minute when Liam O'Brien, a young Irish lad in midfield for United, crunched into Saints' full-back Mark Dennis with such force it split his shin pad in two. With the crowd in uproar and tempers ready to flare, the referee sent O'Brien off. The time on the clock was just eighty-five seconds and it goes down as one of the quickest red cards ever seen. With the kind of red-tinted hindsight with which the world of football would soon become familiar, Fergie later said, 'It was a harsh decision.'

With United out of the way, I know we all had our sights set on reaching Wembley. It hadn't been that long ago that Southampton, then a Second Division club, had beaten United to win the FA Cup; and there had also been a losing League Cup final against Forest, so the fans might be forgiven for sensing another trip up to London was on the cards. But for the second season in a row we came up against Liverpool at the semi-final stage. A year earlier, we had played them in the FA Cup semi-final at White Hart Lane on a rain-sodden pitch in a game that could have gone either way. There was no winner after ninety minutes so the game went into extra time. Two goals from Ian Rush did for us and Liverpool went on to an all-Merseyside Wembley final against Everton.

So, twelve months on and yet another semi-final, this time in the League Cup, but once again there would be no fairy tale for Southampton and it would be my old club that would pull the rug from under us. There had been a considerable turnover at Liverpool since my day – I think there was only Alan Hansen and Kenny Dalglish remaining from the regulars I played with – and of course Kenny, who was player-manager, had to go and score one of the goals as they put us out 3–0.

Liverpool were still the yardstick for any team to measure

themselves against, just as in the late 1970s when I was at Anfield. While at The Dell I was a Southampton player, heart and soul, but no one could ever take away those achievements from my days at Liverpool... even though Mick Mills did try.

We were on an end-of-season trip to the West Indies and Lawrie McMenemy decided I should room with Millsy. He was older than me, by about five years, and an England inter-national of course, so perhaps Lawrie thought he was the best person to keep an eye on me, considering my reputation. Totally unfair, you understand, but I just got on with it. One night, we headed off for a few drinks at a local bar and Mick came out, all dressed up and looking suave in his white jacket, his hair slicked back. He'd got one of those thin cigars on the go and a gin and tonic in his hand, really looking the part.

As the drinks were going down, Mick started banging on about the good old days he had had at Ipswich when they won the Cup and then finished second to Liverpool in the League. Of course, those were the same days when Liverpool were winning the League almost every season, three European Cups, League Cups, charity shields... well, you know the story. Suddenly, Mick turned to me and said, 'You know that team at Liverpool in the late seventies, if you go man for man and compare that team with the Ipswich team, man for man, we were better than you!'

I didn't react, just quietly sipped my beer and said, 'You might be right, Mick, but we won the trophies, you didn't.' Then he said it again, 'Yeah, I know that, but on paper we were the better team, man for man.' And so I reminded him once again that it was the trophies that counted and compared to us, Ipswich had won next to nothing. Still he wouldn't let it drop and this ridiculous conversation went on and on until finally I had had enough. 'Whatever you say, Mick,' I answered, and I picked up my beer and walked off.

I put it down to the banter that bubbles up whenever footballers are together. It doesn't mean anything and it's soon forgotten. I think the best example of that I can come up with is the time I bumped into Terry Phelan just as I was going into a wine bar in Manchester. Terry, who was a little terrier of a full-back, joined me for a drink and we were soon going over old times. He remembered coming up against me when he was playing for Wimbledon and I was at Southampton.

Terry told me that at half-time he had gone into their dressing room and pulled up his shirt to show Vinnie Jones three bright red stud marks across his ribs. 'Who the fuck did that?' said Vinnie. As they poured iodine on the wounds, Terry replied through gritted teeth, 'Who do you fucking think?', leaving no one in any doubt that I was the culprit. As for any hard feelings, not a chance, though: we had a couple of pints and then Terry invited me to his kid's christening party the next day. I couldn't make it, but I appreciated the offer.

I had a similar coming together with John Gorman, in a charity match somewhere, and after the game we were in the bar when he suddenly lifted up his trouser leg and pointed to his shin. 'See that scar? That was you.' I didn't attempt to deny the accusation, I just said, 'Well, John, I was a ball winner and things like that happen. What that scar means is that you must have been playing well to catch my eye.'

'Oh, yeah,' says John, and before you knew it, he was thanking me for saying he was the best player on the pitch.

I didn't mind having that sort of reputation, often it made opposition players a little bit wary, perhaps keeping half an eye on me instead of on the ball, and any advantage you could gain was always worth the effort.

Andy Gray was another player who enjoyed the physical side of the game, always looking to be aggressive and put himself about. I remember one game when he came back from his normal position on the shoulder of our defenders and strayed into my territory. I kind of guessed he was aiming to put his mark on me so I kept an eye on him and when he made his move, I was ready. There is a way of holding yourself when a physical challenge is coming your way and I just had to make sure it was Andy who came off worst – and he did, with a rather painful scrape up the inside of his leg. I walked away, satisfied I had done my job, but he was like a wounded animal, charging around until, finally, he went in once too many times and finished up being stretchered off. I glanced across and gave him a little wave, 'Bye, bye, Andy. Bye, bye.'

As far as I was concerned, and for Andy as well, I reckon, that was all part and parcel of the game: you gave as good as you got. But there have been times when the physical stuff did cross the line. I am thinking especially of a game at Highbury between Southampton and Arsenal when their midfield player, a quiet, talented lad named Paul Davis, did a real number on Glenn Cockerill. The two of them had been having a verbal battle all afternoon and to this day I don't know who said what to whom, but out of the blue, and on the blind side of the referee, Davis came up behind Cockerill and punched him flush on the jaw. The referee missed the attack, but it left Glenn with a broken jaw and definitely affected our play. We had gone 2–0 up but the incident shook us and Arsenal came back to win with a late penalty.

It was their chance to get back in the game – but also my chance to redress the balance with Mr Davis. If the referee wasn't going to take action, then I felt it was up to me to take the appropriate retribution. You can watch how it unfolded on YouTube. As Brian Marwood ran in to take the penalty, I can be spotted coming up behind Davis and drawing my foot back. The camera missed the subsequent moment when I hacked Davis's legs from under him. That was my version of justice but later it was carried out officially when Davis's crime was reviewed on television by the FA: he was fined £3,000 and given a hefty nine-match ban. Fortunately, the referee didn't spot my bit of punishment and it wasn't clear on television, so that was the end of the matter.

I didn't much care for brushes with authority. Playing for Liverpool, I was never sent off and the couple of times later on that I got a red card hardly stand examination. One was a game at Old Trafford for Southampton. They had just brought in the 'last man' rule and I was tracking Bryan Robson as he was going towards goal. There wasn't much contact but Robbo lost his balance and went down. George Courtney came running up, eager to produce a card, but I couldn't believe it when I saw it was red. Kevin Moore was also coming in for a tackle so I was definitely not the so-called 'last man' but George made his decision and refused to review it afterwards.

Another sending-off came in a game for Brighton at Leicester. We were three goals up, with two minutes to go. Already I had been booked in the first half, for handball, when we got a corner. I was waiting for Jeff Minton to come across after he'd been told by the referee to go to the touchline and remove his necklace – with two minutes left, for heaven's sake! I didn't hear the ref telling me to hurry up because I hadn't got my hearing aid in. Anyhow, the ref decided I was time-wasting, produced another yellow card, and that was that: I was sent off and that meant a suspension. I hated that, having to miss games I could never get back.

I didn't see the justice in that dismissal, but I did hold my hand up when there was a strange case of mistaken identity, involving myself and a team-mate who was one of Southampton's budding England internationals. It happened on a trip to play Newcastle at St James's Park in December 1985, a fairly typical First Division game with both sides going at it, hammer and tongs. There was a bit of a crowd scene on the edge of the Newcastle area as players fought for possession so I decided to sort things out with a sliding tackle, which took the ball but took two Newcastle players in the process.

It left one of the Newcastle players on the turf, clutching his injured leg, and suddenly everyone was at each other's throats so I trotted quietly back into midfield and left it to the referee, David Allison, to sort out. Unfortunately, he chose the wrong player to caution. It should have been me, but instead he booked my team-mate and as it was his second yellow card, he had to go.

The sending-off was not going to do the lad's international hopes any good so I offered to help Southampton fight the case with the FA in a bid to get the second yellow card rescinded on the grounds of mistaken identity. The date for the hearing quickly came around and my young team-mate and myself, along with the referee, duly attended the hearing at Lancaster Gate, in front of four old duffers sitting there in judgment in their crisp, dark blazers. The hearing began and we were asked to stand side by side in the dock and the clerk of the hearing said to me, 'Right, Jimmy, you can state your case,' so I said in a stern and clear voice, 'We are stating a case of MISTAKEN IDENTITY.' I was standing next to Danny Wallace, who just happens to be eight inches smaller than me... and is black! It was comical to see all four judges look across at the referee and wonder how the hell he got that one wrong.

At that time there were referees around who you could have a bit of banter with during a game, but there were others who loved to be the centre of attention and were always looking for an excuse to pull out a card. Because of the way I played, I was an easy target and I would do anything to try to avoid a booking, even altering my appearance now and again to throw them off the scent. Short hair, long hair, moustache or clean-shaven, I would always be ringing the changes.

One referee in particular always seemed to have it in for me. He was a little bald-headed Welsh bloke called Keith Cooper. I remember him taking a game at Anfield and after my first iffy tackle, I could see him starting to make his way over and then stop, perhaps thinking it hadn't been bad enough to warrant a card. The second time I transgressed, Mr Cooper repeated the action, once again stopping short of a caution. So after the third borderline challenge, I knew there would be no escape. I was just picking myself up off the turf when Cooper ran over to me, notebook in hand. But I had one last trick up my sleeve, or in my sock, to be accurate. From the top of my bright red Liverpool sock I pulled out a pencil – 'Here you go, ref, use my pencil.' Sadly, the attempt at humour fell on deaf ears because Mr Cooper, using his own pencil, put my name in his little black book.

I can think of only one occasion when a bit of Scouse humour actually worked with a referee. It was with Southampton. I was captain by then and I had to do the coin toss so I was wearing a hearing aid but once we had decided who was going to kick-off, I took it out and put it down in my jock strap for safe keeping because we had no pockets in our shorts. The reason for this was that if it started raining, or I was sweating heavily, the moisture could cause the hearing aid to start crackling like a badly tuned radio. It was another of those tasty encounters with plenty of action in the middle of the park and, inevitably, I suppose, I went in for a tackle that might just have been a millisecond late and the referee decided it was worthy of a caution.

As he came running towards me, I held my hand up, palm facing towards him, as if to say, 'Halt and wait', and he stopped in his tracks. At that moment I reached into my shorts, took out my hearing aid, put it in my ear, switched it on and then said to the ref, 'What?'

He broke out in a big, broad grin, took one look at me and said, 'Fuck off, Jimmy, will ya. Don't do it again!'

CHAPTER TEN

NEXT STOP, BOURNEMOUTH

At Southampton, the years rolled by all too quickly. Six years and two hundred and twenty games had taken me to the age of thirty-seven. I had been a professional footballer for more than twenty years but I never gave any thought to retiring. In fact, my relationship with Chris Nicholl was so good I could see my career developing further at The Dell. We trusted each other, him as my manager, me as captain on the field, and we'd talked about the next logical step, which would have seen me join the coaching staff while signing another one-year playing contract.

I still felt fit enough to contribute on the field but I realised it couldn't last much longer, not at Division One level, and the prospect of passing on some of my experience in a coaching capacity certainly appealed. I might not have had any coaching badges at all – in fact, my milkman, who has not played football to any decent level, is more qualified to coach a football team according to the badges he has got, but I had seventeen years of first team football, mostly at the highest level, under my belt. But as so often happens in football, things changed overnight. The Southampton directors decided that fourteenth place in Division One was not good enough so they sacked Chris Nicholl, the man who brought through Le Tissier, Shearer and Rod Wallace and spotted the potential of a teenage goalkeeper named Tim Flowers; the manager who had kept them safely in Division One for six years, when they got ideas above their station.

In the modern game six years is a long time for a manager to hold down his job at one club, but Southampton always prided itself on back room stability. Chris was only the third manager they had had in thirty-six seasons, following Lawrie McMenemy and the legendary Ted Bates. In my opinion, they should have stuck with Chris, but once the decision to sack him had been made, it became all too easy to ditch under-performing managers and since then, Southampton FC's reception area has resembled a Job Centre with a queue of different managers filing in and out – at the last count it was twenty-two in twenty-three years. It has become one of the hottest seats in football.

From the outset it was clear that the new man, Ian Branfoot, and me weren't going to get along: we just didn't see eye to eye. He took over in June 1991 and it didn't take long for him to lay his cards on the table when he called me into his office and explained that he was going to change the team's playing style from the passing game Chris Nicholl had adopted to a long ball game. Branfoot wanted the back line to get it up and forward as quickly as possible and then try to win the second ball on the edge of the opposition penalty area. For that he needed players who could get up and down the pitch. He looked me straight in the eye and said that, at the age of thirty-seven, he didn't think it was a job I could do.

Well, to be perfectly honest, it was a job I *didn't want* to do. I hate that kick-and-rush style of football, where the ball spends more time in the air than it does on the deck. It is neither attractive nor very successful, and I didn't want any part of it.

Having established the fact that we had very different views about the game and how it should be played, Branfoot reached the moment when he had to tell me he was dispensing with my services. The way he put it made it sound as if he was doing me a favour. 'I would like to give you a free transfer,' he said, meaning that I could go and find another club with no fee involved.

'You want to give me a free transfer?' I replied. 'Let me tell you that I have been at this club for longer than five years and I am over the age of thirty-five, and that means I am *entitled* to a free transfer whether you want me to go or not. So let's get this straight, you have given me fuck-all!' On that note I said, 'See you,' and walked out of his office and away from Southampton FC.

But I had done some research of my own on Mr Branfoot, by phoning a few friends of mine who had played at the club, or clubs where he had been a player, coach or manager, and the same theme came back to me: that they all thought he was an arrogant man. I shouldn't have been surprised at the way things turned out. I'm sure Branfoot came in with some words of advice from various people about getting rid of the older, more influential players in the dressing room, and the fact that local newspaper polls were calling for me to get Chris Nicholl's job would have put him on his guard. In his book the name Jimmy Case would have spelt trouble so he did what he had to do.

He made a big deal out of the transfer in the newspapers, about how he was helping me out by giving me the chance to continue my career lower down the League. But I know for sure, that wasn't how the Southampton fans saw the situation. It was only a year since they'd voted me Player of the Season and I know I was the popular choice to take over from Chris. Still, that didn't happen and I was never one for looking back and wondering what might have been. The only question in my mind was: where next for me? I wasn't ready to hang up my boots and I couldn't see any good reason why I should. With all my experience, I could still do a job for someone but the question was: Who would take a chance on a thirty-seven-year-old? Harry Redknapp, that's who!

Harry was just down the coast at Bournemouth, where he had begun to establish his reputation as a first-class manager. It had been his first job in management and he'd been there for the best part of eight years, winning a promotion and proving he was an ace motivator and a guy who knew how to make a good deal for the club. Within an hour of the news coming out that I'd been released by Southampton, he was on the phone, inviting me to meet him for a chat. It sounded good to me: if I liked what Harry had to say, I could carry on playing football and wouldn't have to travel very far to do it. We met at Rownhams Services on the M27 and within an hour the deal was done and I became a Bournemouth player. It was in the same close season for Bournemouth that Harry's son Jamie left the club to go to Liverpool, and what a player he was... and also a top bloke.

Bournemouth had slipped back into the Third Division and Harry told me his plan was to go for promotion the next season with younger players, but he needed an experienced minder in midfield, someone who could boss the centre of the park with enough ability to pull the young lads together; I remember he said something about stopping other teams taking liberties. Well, that kind of scenario suited me perfectly.

That season I played forty-nine times for Bournemouth, alongside Kevin Bond, and while I've never been one to bear grudges, I couldn't help thinking about Ian Branfoot's words when he suggested that I wouldn't play much now I was thirty-seven. I just felt it was a shame that he didn't try to get to know me a bit better and take the time to see if I could have helped his cause rather than hinder it, as he seemed to think. And one thing that happened certainly didn't help: the Southampton fans turned on him for letting me go. Branfoot lasted less than three seasons and the best he did for Southampton was to get them to the final of the Zenith Data Systems Cup when his team, with Shearer, Le Tissier, Benali, Cockerill, Iain Dowie, Barry Horne, Kevin Moore and Tim Flowers in goal, lost to Forest. It was the highlight of his managerial career.

Down at Bournemouth, the atmosphere was comfortable, much more homely, the ambitions more realistic and achievable. The people there were good, hard-working types, with an ingrained love of the club. I could sympathise with that sort of attitude and I settled in quickly.

There was an old chap whose job it was to cut the grass. He kept his lawnmower and tins of white paint in a little den underneath the main stand and many a time I would wander in and sit for hours, just chatting about this and that. He liked a tot of whisky and would ask if I wanted a wee dram. My reply was always the same, 'I will, if you will.'

They had another bloke, Ken Sullivan, who was known as 'Nimbus'. He was responsible for running the gear up to the training ground and back. They were mundane, thankless jobs, but these fellas did it because they loved the club and I always tried to help them when I could. It was the least they deserved.

We trained down near Bournemouth Airport with Harry and his assistant, Tony Pulis, who was also on the playing staff that season. Tony's mantra was 'fitness, fitness, fitness'. All he wanted was to run everybody off their feet to get them ready for games. Now, I've nothing against that but you have to understand that at my age most players have had enough of running up sand hills and, to be perfectly honest, it was not what I needed. All that was required was to put the ball at my feet and let me take it from there. Surround me with some young legs and you had the perfect blend. But I'm not having a go at Tony; he was always very, very enthusiastic and I'm sure nothing has changed. I am not surprised he has gone on to do good things as a manager. He could be a hard task-master, but he also enjoyed a laugh and could always get players wanting to play for him. I look at what he did to turn Crystal Palace round and I know nothing has changed.

Harry Redknapp was pretty much the same. He could blow his top, for sure. One minute he would say you were rubbish and the next he had his arm round your shoulder, telling you how good you were. He never held a grudge and he has a superb football brain. I think he would have made a terrific England manager because players instantly warm to him, and he has a good relationship with other managers. But, a little like Cloughie before him, Harry comes with a bit of baggage and that frightened the FA. Maybe one day they will give the job to the best manager instead of the best diplomat, but then again, maybe not.

I was only at Bournemouth for a season and I found the Third Division a real eye-opener. It was a completely different level to anything I had experienced before but I didn't mind that. I had always thrived on being given different challenges, being put in situations that made you think about the game and I could see another season at least, especially after the fans voted me Player of the Season.

It was during that season, an away game at West Bromwich Albion, that I played my 550th League match – more than seven hundred matches when you add in all the cups – and I can honestly say I was enjoying it just as much as when I started. I was thirty-eight years old, captain of a decent team, and pushing for promotion... what more could I ask for?

For much of that season it looked as if we might go up and

if we had pulled it off it would have given me as much satisfaction as anything I have ever achieved. People used to tell me it was 'only' the Third Division – so what? The chance to win something, no matter what kind of trophy, should not be dismissed by any player. In the end, we missed out by a few points but looking back, it still adds up to one of the most enjoyable periods of my career.

Well, there was one dark moment. I was sent off in a home game against Shrewsbury Town. Now I have never been one to argue with referees; as far as I am concerned, it is a complete waste of time. I cannot remember an incident in which a ref has changed his mind because players have told him he had made a mistake but Roger Wiseman got that one wrong. It was a 50–50 challenge for the ball, with Shrewsbury player Mark Taylor, the sort I had been making for twenty years. I got there first and he went down in a heap – a bit theatrical, to say the least.

Perhaps it was my reputation that got me sent off but it was a nothing incident and I was steaming as I took the long walk back to the dressing room. After the match Harry Redknapp was fuming and the club immediately sent in an appeal to the FA. There was video of the incident that seemed to show there was no intentional contact and Harry was confident we would win. Well, needless to say, the FA saw it differently. That cost me a three-game suspension at a time in my career when I didn't want to miss a single match. I knew the end of my playing days was getting ever closer but I still lived for my football and every game was precious to me.

And it wasn't just the football. I enjoyed being involved in everything around the club and at Dean Court I was able to muck in, even though it raised a few eyebrows. I will never forget the look on our kit man Ken Sullivan's face after we had lost a friendly against Fareham Town and he walked into the changing room to see me picking up all the dirty kit ready for the wash, and then pouring out teas for the lads. I don't think he was used to seeing players do that sort of thing. It was just a natural thing for me to do, something Bill Shankly taught me. He would tell us that if we could help someone in any way, we should do it, and that included rolling up our kit after games to make it easier for the apprentices and the kit man to collect. They were lessons in life that I have taken with me wherever I have played, lessons learnt from Shanks and the other members of staff at Liverpool. It was always about a team effort off the pitch as well as on it.

I fancied another year or two at Dean Court to finish off my career. On the field I was still doing the business, but away from it the business was not good. The banks moved in and started looking at ways to cut costs. I was on a one-year contract and it was all too easy to dispense with my services. The same thing happened to Kevin Bond who, incidentally, had been voted the Away Player of the Year.

Harry Redknapp and the club chairman came round to my house in Chandlers Ford and as we sat having a cup of tea, he told me they couldn't afford to renew my contract. Times must have been hard because I wasn't on that much money anyway – I really was just playing for the love of it. Money was never a great issue for me. In twenty years as a player I never had a dispute with a manager over wages. I even offered to play for half my salary to make things easier with the banks, but the truth of the matter was they wanted to strip the finances down to the bone and I had to go.

I knew I would miss the atmosphere at Dean Court. I've played for top clubs in the biggest games, but down at Bournemouth the support was tremendous, something I will never forget. And hearing Harry say I was the last player that he wanted to let go didn't help much either; perhaps it even made the situation worse. It was a blow, that's for sure. I wanted to carry on playing for as long as I could and I knew the only way to do that was to keep up my fitness levels by getting games.

Harry suggested that at my age I should ease up on the training and that was good advice, but I didn't want to give up playing. Once you stop, at that age, it is difficult, if not impossible, to rebuild your fitness so I went home and sat by the phone, waiting for the offers to come flooding in. And I sat there, and I sat there, gazing through the patio windows for hours on end, watching the leaves blowing across my lawn. For the first time since I was eighteen, I didn't have a club. For more than twenty years I had gone into the close season knowing that training would soon begin again. But now I was bored, with little prospect of a game of footy to lift my spirits.

Then, at last, the telephone rang. 'Hi Jimmy, what are you up to these days?' said a familiar voice on the other end of the line. It was Frank Worthington. We had played together at Brighton, and shared a room on away trips, and although he was the complete opposite to me, we had always got on.

What you saw was what you got with Frank: flamboyant, just as likely to be in the papers with a Page Three girl as he was for scoring goals. And he did plenty of that because he was one of the most skilful players to grace the game.

'Not a lot,' I replied, wondering – and hoping – about what was coming next.

'How do you fancy coming up to Halifax and playing some football?'

Have boots, will travel! Next thing you know I'm on a train heading for deepest Yorkshire to meet up with Frank, who was helping out Halifax manager John McGrath with a bit of coaching. McGrath had been a player before my time but I knew 'Big Jake' by reputation as a tough, no-nonsense sort of guy. Old school like me, and that was good enough. On training mornings in Halifax it was bitterly cold, even in pre-season August, and I was there in the winter months of October and November. My God, it was cold! I remember the players would put Deep Heat on their arms and legs before going out training.

Well, one morning I saw Big Jake putting some of this Deep Heat on, rubbing it into his arms and legs. What he had left on his hands he would rub into his face, behind his ears, then proceed to give his privates a coating of the stuff. What a man!

We met up at The Shay and John offered to take me to lunch in the club diner. I was ready to sign there and then, any sort of contract, but I got the impression he felt he had to sell the idea to me and so he launched into his after-dinner routine. Bloody hell, he was good, but he didn't half go on... and on... and on, until the afternoon and half the evening had passed before we got round to talking turkey. The contract was for a year, with me agreeing to travel up to Halifax three or four days a week and stay at a local hotel on a sponsorship deal. It suited me, I just wanted to keep on playing, and an added bonus was that Frank would be there and I knew he was a good drinking partner.

There were more than enough pubs around Halifax to satisfy our thirst – not that we went in every one of them, of course – and I got to like the town. The weather might not be the best up there; someone once tried to explain to me, over a couple of pints, that it was something to do with Halifax being in a valley. It didn't really sink in.

At that level of football we had a half-decent side and we were getting the results to match. I was visiting places I'd never been to before, like Stockport and Rochdale and one or two other sunspots of the North. It was fun, but once again money reared its ugly head and that meant more problems for James Robert Case.

Something happened between the hotel owners and the club. I soon cottoned on that they were trying to ease me out when they moved me to a different room, right over the function suite. It just happened to coincide with Christmas and there were a few discos going on down there. They must have thought the noise would be enough to drive me out. Of course, they had no idea it wouldn't bother me... I just took out my hearing aid and got my head down!

In the end I left it up to the club and the hotel to sort out their differences while I moved into the centre of town, into some rooms over a wine bar run by two Polish lads, Zoran and his mate, whose name escapes me right now. It was a little corner of heaven, with plenty of booze on tap, a nice atmosphere off the field and I was still getting regular football. I got twenty-one games for Halifax under my belt when it all went belly-up. John McGrath left, Frank Worthington wasn't around much, and Halifax appeared to be heading for the non-league wilderness. I was beginning to wonder how long I could keep my career going when out of the blue I got a telephone call from another old mate.

This time it was Joey Jones, the lad I had first roomed with all those years ago at Liverpool. He had gone back to Wales, to his favourite club, Wrexham. Brian Flynn was manager and his assistant was Kevin Reeves, who I played against when he was at Norwich and Manchester City, and who is now chief scout at Everton. Kevin picked me up from Crewe railway station and took me to his house, where I stayed overnight. We sat and talked football into the early hours and he outlined everything to me about what Flynn was planning. It was all about the club adding another experienced player to their ranks in case of injury or suspension because they were going for promotion at the time.

Even though I only played four games, I was there from February 1993 to the end of the season and I enjoyed every minute. They had a great dressing room, full of characters; great atmosphere and the supporters were brilliant. But the bottom line was that I was looking for yet another club and I was starting to run out of options. There were a few irons in the fire, but one opportunity I had certainly never considered was the town of Kingsley, Perth, Western Australia, and a football club called Wanneroo British. Still, I was always prepared to go anywhere for a game and twelve thousand miles to the other side of the world didn't seem a bad idea at the time.

It was an ex-pro named John Sydenham who made it happen: he had played at Southampton during the Terry Paine era and then emigrated to Perth, where he got involved with an ex-pats team full of Scousers and Geordies called Wanneroo British. He was back in Southampton in 1993 when we met and he asked me if I would like to come out for five or six weeks and play a few games for them.

Sounds simple, but with me still a full-time professional, I had to sign international forms, explain myself to the Australian immigration people and tell them why I was there. It was all good experience and the life out there was fun in the sun. This was never going to be a permanent thing, more a paid holiday, really. I was contracted to turn out as a guest player for Wanneroo British and during my month out there I played four games, trained with the team two nights a week but then it was back to England.

When I got home I got another call, to turn out for a Yorkshire non-league team called North Ferriby United in an FA Cup game, but that never happened – because I couldn't get international clearance!

What came next was a single game for Darlington. I am always getting asked, why only one game? It was the usual story. They had just sacked their manager and my mate, Gerry Forrest from Southampton days, had taken over as caretaker. His first job was to find a replacement for his main midfield player Neil McNab, who had joined Derry Town in Ireland, so he asked if I would help him out. Of course I said yes.

I drove up to Darlington from Southampton on the Friday, stayed in a local hotel and then played against Wycombe Wanderers, who at the time were going well under manager Martin O'Neill. We drew the game, the team did quite well and I travelled back down south, thinking there would be more to come. But on the Monday Gerry became the latest in a long line of short-term managers at Darlington when he was relieved of his position and that, as they say, was that – the end of another brief episode of my career.

It seemed to signal the end of my Football League career. Where else could I go? But the thing was, I still felt fit enough and enthusiastic enough to keep going and I refused to hang up my boots. So I saw nothing wrong in signing for an ex-pro named John Ryan, who was manager at Sittingbourne, then a half-decent Southern League team. From where I was standing, it seemed like it would be a nice gentle way to bring the curtain down on more than twenty years of playing the game I loved. But there was one more unexpected twist to come in the Jimmy Case story and, in many ways, it would turn out to be the most dramatic chapter of all.

It all started, as so often happens, with a telephone call. On the line was my old 1983 FA Cup final buddy Gerry Ryan with an invitation that almost knocked me off my feet. 'Hi Jimmy, how do you fancy coming back to play for Brighton?'

Over the years I had played for nine different clubs but as you might have guessed, there were three that became a huge part of my life: Liverpool, Southampton... and Brighton. I had been through a lot of different experiences with the Seagulls and the chance to return to the Goldstone, perhaps to relive old glories, rekindle a few memories, was too good to turn down, especially now I was tip-toeing past forty years of age. It was also a chance to work with a player I had always admired, the great Arsenal star Liam Brady, who had just taken over as manager, with Gerry his assistant. With barely a moment's hesitation I said yes.

But it wasn't the same Brighton I had left in the mid-1980s. I had missed the club's descent towards the bottom of Division Two and into a world of financial misery during the latter part of the decade and then into the nineties, a time when they had been a heartbeat away from being wound up because they couldn't pay their debts, with the taxman leading the queue of creditors. The club had been saved first by selling off a couple of their best players and then, around the time I re-signed, by a couple of wealthy directors named Bill Archer and Greg Stanley, who had apparently stumped up nearly £1m to keep their head above water. Little did anyone know at the time that the cash was not quite what it seemed and their agenda wasn't wholly for the benefit of Brighton and Hove Albion FC.

Archer, a DIY tycoon who lived in Blackburn, and his business partner Stanley appointed a new CEO named David Bellotti and they had brought in Liam Brady to run the team. This seemed to answer all the fans' prayers as the board started talking about redeveloping the Goldstone as a retail park, bringing in much-needed finance, but not until they had found a new ground. It all sounded good to me but at that stage I was more than happy to let the accountants sort out all that kind of thing. I was excited by the offer from Liam: to play first team football again, but also to look after the reserves alongside the ex-West Ham veteran, George Petchey. The idea was that if everything worked out OK, there would be a permanent place on the staff for me. I hadn't thought much about what I would do once I finished playing, but if it could involve coaching youngsters and passing on some of my experience, I was more than interested.

I returned to the Goldstone with my boots polished, my motivation as high as it had ever been and with a genuine belief that my life in football was far from over. On the field, it all started well: results were beginning to improve; I was getting a few games and enjoying my work with the second string. It was all about the football, as far as I was concerned. George and I would run our eyes over the reserves and then report back to Liam and Gerry about who might, or might not, make it to the first team. Those meetings were usually held over a bowl of pasta at Topolino's restaurant in Hove and during one lunchtime chat Liam asked if I had ever had a testimonial or benefit game.

I told him I had spent nine years at Liverpool, one short of the stipulated ten needed to qualify for a testimonial, so it had never happened. But he reckoned that after twenty years as a professional, with a few cups and medals in my collection, I certainly deserved one. That, as far as I was concerned, was that: it was just a chat over lunch. But a few days later, Liam called me into his office and told me he had been on the phone to Roy Evans, then manager at Liverpool, to ask him about bringing a Liverpool team down to Brighton to play a benefit match for me. Roy had given the idea the thumbs-up but could only find one date on the Liverpool calendar: Monday, 17 October 1994. To say I was gob-smacked would be an understatement. I had known nothing about any of this, it was all down to Liam... but it meant I had only a few weeks to set up a committee and get things organised.

A Monday night fixture has never been regarded as the best night to play a benefit match, but I needn't have worried. The Brighton fans snapped up every ticket, and why wouldn't they? Roy Evans sent down the whole first team, including his big stars: John Barnes, Ian Rush, Robbie Fowler, Steve McManaman, Jamie Redknapp... And I managed to persuade Matt Le 'God' Tissier to pull on a Brighton shirt for a one-night appearance.

The ground was packed to the rafters and I cannot explain my feelings when I ran out. There was a guard of honour from both sides and the air was filled with fans chanting my name. That night there was a real mixture of emotions and, I can admit it now, for the first time in my career I was really nervous. I had played in FA Cup finals, won European Cups, but that was different. It had all been about the team then, but that night in October 1994 was all about me and I wasn't used to it, I wasn't quite sure how to handle it. Still, it was a marvellous night. Liverpool won 2–1, and after the game we all retired to the Grand Hotel, where I had organised a reception with plenty of food, and plenty of drinks. I quickly discovered that the current Liverpool squad wasn't so different from my day... they all liked a pint or two!

As the night wore on, the numbers dwindled until only a

few diehards were left in the bar. I was there, but that goes without saying, and so too was Ian Rush, Robbie Fowler, Roy Evans, David Moores, the Liverpool chairman, and the Reds' goalkeeper, David James. I am not sure what prompted the comment, but I suddenly turned to James and said, 'I don't fucking rate you as a goalkeeper anyway. After two seasons you'll be up the road.' Now I know everyone round the table heard me, but James chose to ignore the jibe, so I was just going to leave it when I felt a tap on my leg and Rushy leaned over. 'Go on, Jim, tell him again!' That's footballers for you, anything to stir things up or get a laugh. Just like kids, they never grow up.

It turned out to be one of the best nights of my career, a special memory, and I cannot thank Liam, Brighton and Hove Albion FC, Roy Evans and Liverpool enough for making it happen. At that moment there was no doubt in my mind that the opportunity to go back to the Goldstone had come with a perfect sense of timing.

But the romance was about to turn sour, in more ways than one.

CHAPTER ELEVEN

TIME TO CALL IT A DAY

I was forty-one years, five months and twenty-one days old when I announced that my career as a professional footballer had come to an end. I hadn't really thought about how I would bow out, but it would have been nice to play my final game in front of a decent crowd and leave the field with one last wave to the fans, my head held high. But instead my career came crashing to a close in a Football Combination fixture between Brighton Reserves and Arsenal Reserves watched by a handful of silent supporters.

Inevitably, I suppose, it was the result of a typically strong challenge, but for once I came off worst as I fell heavily on my neck. I heard something crack and for a few moments I was paralysed. I genuinely thought I had broken my neck and for just about the first time in my life, I was frightened to death.

When I hit the floor I couldn't feel anything from the neck

down and just lay there, looking up at all these concerned faces. Someone shouted for a stretcher and then the club physio, Malcolm Stuart, and the club doctor, Herzl Sless, came on and very gently started to examine me. I don't know how long it took before I started to get some feeling back into my right hand and my right leg: maybe seconds, maybe a few minutes.

They lifted me onto the stretcher and that's when the feeling started to return to my left side and I breathed a huge sigh of relief. I was rushed off to hospital with a surgical collar round my neck and taken for X-rays, which revealed I hadn't broken any bones and I was going to be all right. But it had shaken me up, physically and mentally; I felt like I'd been hit on the back of the head with a big mallet. I couldn't lift my head off the pillow, or turn to look over my shoulder. And as I lay there in that hospital bed I did some serious thinking.

I had to face up to the fact that I was getting a bit too old to compete against tough young players who hadn't been born when I made my Liverpool debut. They didn't care that I was the oldest outfield player in the game; my medals meant nothing to them. And that was how it had to be if they were going to make it. It was time for me to get out of their way.

When I got back to the Goldstone I sat down with Liam Brady and we had a long chat about the future. Reluctantly, but realistically, I listened to his advice and decided that was it. More than twenty years had passed since I had made my League debut for Liverpool against Queens Park Rangers and suddenly it was all over. Where had the time gone?

But it didn't take me long to come to terms with things. It

helped that I was coaching the reserves at Brighton so my involvement didn't change much. These days there is a lot of emphasis on coaching badges and that type of thing, but I didn't have any and I didn't fancy going through all the rigmarole to get them. No one had badges at Liverpool. I think Bob Paisley had a paper for physiotherapy, but that was about it. I watch players now and get frustrated when they don't play to a particular standard. Having to work with them year in, year out would have been too much for me; I couldn't have done it. I was comfortable working with the reserves and didn't see myself taking it much further, but what happened next was beyond my control.

Behind the scenes it was all starting to kick off as the true nature of Archer and Stanley's intentions became clear. Liam was trying to run the team against a background of surveys and planning applications for a new ground, but they turned out to be nothing more than a smokescreen: it was all about selling the Goldstone. The deal Archer and Stanley had done, apparently to save the club, had actually been a loan from the bank, using the Goldstone as collateral. Their intention was to flog the club and leave with their money. Of course the fans were up in arms when the ground was eventually sold to a development company. Archer, Stanley and the rest of the board said they had done it to clear mounting debts, but the move came as a bombshell, with no plans and no site for a new home for the club.

Into the picture came Dick Knight, a local businessman and diehard Brighton fan, who laid out his plans to take over the club. Liam Brady committed himself to Knight and his consortium, and in that situation he decided he had little option but to resign as manager. That's when he gave me the call that shook my world.

'Hi Jimmy, I am going to quit,' he told me, 'and I think they will probably turn to you to take over.'

That took the wind out of my sails, I can tell you. It was hardly the most attractive managerial job in football, and I didn't want to appear disloyal to Liam. I had enjoyed my time with him and for my money he was one of the best managers I had ever worked with. He had begun to turn Brighton around and to be honest, I felt sick for him. I got him to agree that if I took it on, as soon as Dick Knight's consortium took over he would come back. It sounded like a plan, but we had all reckoned without Bill Archer's refusal to give up control of Brighton.

Given that sort of atmosphere, it was hardly surprising the team got relegated into Division Three. There would be home games where the only man in the directors' box was David Bellotti and he would just sit there, stoney-faced, as the fans hurled all this abuse at him... and also chucked fireworks. I got the impression he had been set up to take all the flak for the absent owners. He was getting chased by angry supporters and even had to have a police escort.

When the final game of the 1995/96 season came around, it seemed the end of the line for Brighton at the Goldstone Ground, which by then was falling down around the club's ears. Talk was all about a ground-sharing arrangement with Portsmouth at Fratton Park, but the fans were having none of it. Brighton entertained York City in what everyone believed would be the last ever game at the Goldstone. The atmosphere was charged with tension, banners read 'sack the board' and 'no move to Pompey'. The game lasted barely fifteen minutes before the supporters invaded the pitch to make sure their protests were heard and the tie was duly abandoned.

Archer and Stanley had been backed into a corner. They were forced to accept a deal with the new owners which would give them another season at the Goldstone, in return for a rent figure the papers said was nearly half a million pounds.

During the next season, as I tried to build a team capable of challenging at the top of the table, the hostility towards the directors and owners was at its highest level. David Bellotti was the only one attending matches and the only one to be seen at the ground during weekdays. On one occasion the supporters' protests threatened to get out of hand when a large group stormed the main stand to try to take over the ground. The atmosphere was decidedly hostile, the teams back in the dressing rooms having been ordered off the pitch by the referee. I told the referee and his officials to stay in their room and I took all the ball boys and girls and put them in the treatment room for safety. At that moment we had riot police in full gear in the players' tunnel trying to keep the fans out. It was bedlam.

All any manager wants from any club is the chance to actually manage but that had become impossible after the way the owners and Bellotti were behaving.

Another incident highlighting the deep troubles at the club occurred during a game at the Goldstone Ground. Brighton were fighting to get some results and 2–1 down and kicking towards our favourite end, we were piling on the pressure in search of an equaliser. There must have been about ten minutes to go when two rockets were set off together into the night sky from the road next to the ground. They exploded high above the ground, two almighty bangs, which was the signal for the latest protest to start. All the fans got to their feet and walked out of the ground. It was nothing to do with the football, just to protest against the board and get the papers talking, but it didn't help the team. That's what we were up against – manager, staff and players – but I don't blame the Brighton supporters for the actions they took. They are as fanatical about their club as any group of fans in the country and they deserved better than they were getting from the owners.

Few clubs can have experienced the turmoil that engulfed Brighton and Hove Albion at that time, with the loss of their ground, having to play home games at Gillingham for two seasons, and then having to play at the Withdean Stadium, a makeshift ground that had been built for athletics. Today, nearly twenty years later, I can honestly say that I'm so made up for all parties concerned, especially the supporters, that they have their new stadium and they are enjoying some good times again.

At the time I did my best under the circumstances. I brought a couple of players in, Ian Baird was one, and tried to win a few games to keep Brighton away from the bottom of the table and the unthinkable prospect of relegation out of the Football League. Out on the pitch the players were trying to win games while the biggest struggle was going on behind the scenes. Everywhere we went the fans were more interested in what was happening to their club than watching games and they made their feelings clear with continual protests against Archer and the board. It was an impossible situation but I stuck it out, hoping the Dick Knight consortium would take over, but it didn't happen quickly enough for me. Then David Bellotti gave me the sack.

But I didn't care. I hadn't wanted the job in the first place and by then I had had more than enough. It had been twenty-four hours a day, seven days a week of stress and as anyone will tell you, I don't handle stress very well. I am far too easy-going to get wrapped up in that sort of an existence, so when I got my P45 it came as something of a relief. There was little doubt in my mind that I was better off out of it.

But the game wouldn't leave me alone; the wheels within wheels in football never stopped turning. A chap named Ray Pinney gave me a call. We had a mutual friend in Steve Foster, who Ray had known from his days as a director at Luton Town. Ray had retired on his money made out of the insurance business and was filling his time as chairman of a local Southern League outfit, Bashley FC, along with a local builder named Trevor Adams. It is blokes like Ray and Trevor who are the lifeblood of football, investing time and money in the grassroots of the game. Without them and hundreds more like them, it would wither and die.

I liked Ray from the off, even though he did drive around in a flash Rolls-Royce! And I got the nod of approval about Ray from Fozzie, so when he suggested I come along to Bashley as manager, I quite liked the idea. I had a part-time role in mind, taking training a couple of times a week and then running the games on a Saturday, which would leave me time to get some fishing in on the River Test, not far from my house in Chandler's Ford. Ray wanted more than that and so, over another of those famous pasta lunches, he finally persuaded me to take it on full-time.

At that time a lad called Barry Blankley was running the team and I wanted to keep him onside because he had a wealth of knowledge about the non-league scene and the standard of players in the area. I needed his help. So we sat down and I spelt it out: my name would be down in the programme notes as manager but we would run the side together. Barry accepted the situation and I am so grateful he did. Especially in the early days when I was getting to know my way around the Southern League, he was invaluable. It was the start of a friendship that has lasted to this day.

Just like most of the steps along the way, my time at Bashley was memorable for all the right reasons. The challenge was just the same as at any other club, it's always about trying to win matches, but I didn't feel the same pressure, certainly not after my Brighton experience. We had a great bunch of lads, including three or four Royal Navy PT instructors, which meant Bashley was one of the fittest teams in the League. Then there were some talented youngsters, like our strikers, Paul Sales and James Taylor, who were the envy of other clubs at our level. There was also another lad who I thought had something a bit extra. He was good at passing, dribbling and although a bit on the short side, he had that aggressive edge to his game which I liked (I'd seen it somewhere before!).

His name cropped up when I played in a charity match at Christchurch FC for a Bournemouth XI, along with other ex-players such as Ted McDougall, John Williams, and John Wark as a guest player. It turned out to be a great night, watched by a decent crowd. As usual, after a shower, we headed up to the club bar for a good chat about old and new times. I turned to John 'Willow' Williams, who was, and still is, a massive character from his time as a player at Bournemouth and then assistant manager to the then boss, Mel Machin, and asked him, 'Some of the younger players who turned out for us tonight, what level are they at?'

'They are in our reserves,' said Willow.

I took the opportunity to tell him we had a good lad at Bashley. 'I think he could more than hold his own with those lads of yours,' I said. 'His name is Wade Elliott.' Fair play to Willow, he liked what he heard and so, between us, we arranged for Wade to take part in a couple of Bournemouth reserve team games in front of Machin. He liked what he saw and offered Wade a full-time contract but that put Wade in a dilemma, just as I myself had faced all those years ago when Liverpool wanted to sign me while I was still doing my electricians' apprenticeship at Evans Medical.

Wade was a bright lad with a place at Loughborough University in the bag, something he wasn't that keen to give up. So I sat him down and suggested he took a year away from his education to give a career in football a go.

'You only get one chance,' I told him, 'and in years to

come, you might be kicking yourself if you don't at least give it a try.'

After talking it over with his family, Wade did sign for Bournemouth. That was in the year 2000 and, at the time of writing, he is still playing, having chalked up more than five hundred games, including a spell in the Premier League, for Bournemouth, Burnley and Birmingham City. I like to think that when he retires, he will look back and decide he did the right thing.

He has Bashley to thank for giving him a long career in the game, just as I could say the same about South Liverpool and me. Non-league football has been a stepping stone for many a good player, just ask John Aldridge, and there are plenty more good lads playing down there who would be well worth a go and might save top clubs a lot of money they would otherwise spend on some here-today, gone-tomorrow import.

The best modern story I can think of, and which should serve as an inspiration to any would-be footballer ever knocked back, is Rickie Lambert at my old club, Liverpool. Rickie is a Merseyside lad who got onto Liverpool's books as a teenager but didn't make the grade and had to start all over again at non-league Marine. He stuck at it, got picked up by Blackpool and then spent a few years trawling around the lower leagues, ending up at Saints at the time when they had just dropped into League One. Everyone knows what happened next: he was part of the Southampton rise to the Premier League, won a place in the England team and now he is living the dream with a big money move back to Liverpool. The icing on the cake came when he was called up by Roy

Hodgson for the World Cup in Brazil. It is a real Roy of the Rovers story, but just a pity that when it came to crunch-time England made such a balls-up.

We will never become a major force unless we develop a mean streak, like the South Americans and the Italians. We are too soft, too honest. It stems from the manager. I have no problem with Roy Hodgson but he is too nice to be an international manager; he was the same at Liverpool. I would much rather have a nasty guy in charge, and then perhaps we might win something. The top managers are sharp, ruthless, cunning – think about the managers who should have had the job, like Cloughie and Harry Redknapp. The best England manager of recent times was Terry Venables, and he could be cute too when it came to tactics.

England should be more like Argentina, Italy or Uruguay. Build a team around your best player, don't shove him out on the wing. And get a foot in early. No one made a tackle on Mario Balotelli, nor Suarez, and look what happened. If they had been getting kicked from pillar to post they might not have found it so easy to be on the spot when the goal chances came around.

I don't think, for one minute, that being an international manager is easy. Far from it. I certainly wouldn't want that sort of pressure. But if you do take it on you have got to do everything possible to get the best out of the talent available – and, for me, Hodgson and all his coaches, psychologists, dieticians etc are going the wrong way about it. I learned that much in my brief time as a manager with Brighton, and at Bashley.

One thing about being manager of a non-league team, you always have to expect the unexpected. You are not dealing with multi-million pound players who have every aspect of their lives organised for them, you are dealing with lads who have nine-to-five jobs and all the complications of life to deal with before they can start to think about pulling on a shirt for a game of footy.

There was the time we were heading off to Kent to play Tonbridge Angels. We had arranged to pick up most of the players at Rownhams Services on the M27 and then we set off on what would be a three-hour round trip. About thirty minutes into the journey one of the players, a cheeky lad named Dave Morris, suddenly piped up, 'Hey, I hope you buggers up the front realise we haven't got a bloody goalkeeper!'

'Don't worry,' I shouted down the coach, 'we'll sort it out when we get there.'

On arrival at the Tonbridge ground, I pulled out a golf cap, took an ordinary pair of gloves and doctored them up with white tape across the knuckle, wrote the brand name 'Reusch' on them in felt tip, and then sat the players down.

'As you know, we don't have a goalkeeper for today's game, so what Barry and I have decided to do is put all the players' names in a hat. The youngest member of the squad will pick one out and whoever is drawn will be between the sticks this afternoon.'

The look on the players' faces was priceless. 'You're having a laugh,' said one, all of them thinking this was a wind-up and expecting our keeper to come walking through the door. Trouble was, he'd been taken ill the night before and our reserve was at work. Ah, the joys of managing in the non-league!

So the draw was made and out came the name of Phil Andrews – who just happened to be our best striker and leading goalscorer. But I had made up the rules so I threw the gloves, cap and keeper's jersey at him and told him to get on with it. The rest of the players thought I was mad, but there was method there. I had brought Phil with me from Brighton Reserves... where he had been quite a decent goalkeeper.

Well, I certainly had the last laugh that day. The trick was that I had written his name on all the pieces of paper that went into the hat. Phil played a blinder, more as a sweeper than a goalie, but he did make two or three top saves as well and we eventually won the game 3–1!

CHAPTER TWELVE

THEN
AND NOW

There are some people who have suggested that I wouldn't last five minutes in the modern game. I don't buy that. What team wouldn't want a player who gives 100 per cent every time he goes onto the pitch, can make an accurate pass short or long, knows the correct way to cross the ball, who has an eye for goal and a thunderbolt shot? That's all well and good, they say, but what about your tackling? You would be sent off every other game. The simple answer is that I would have to adapt and I like to think I was a good enough player to do so.

Rules are rules. They used to change them every season back in my day. The referee would come to the club to explain what was what; it might be an offside thing or it might be the type of tackle that could get you sent off. He told us what was expected and we just had to adapt accordingly. I think there was certainly a bit more leeway with tackling back then. Where a tackle today earns an instant yellow card, back then you would get a warning or two first. But the principles have never changed. We were always taught to stay on our feet as much as possible and then time our tackles to win the ball. Perhaps we had a bit more room to manoeuvre, where we could take the ball and the player at the same time.

They say the game is faster these days, but I don't agree. You can't run the hundred metres any quicker now than you could in my day. We were just as skilful. The Liverpool way was always about control, passing, shooting – intelligent movement off the ball. You had to have something going on above the neck, so what's changed? And remember, when I played the ball was much heavier, boots were heavier, pitches were worse. What we didn't have was all the technical stuff they have today: individual fitness charts, training regimes and special diets designed for different players. Coaches for this, coaches for that; I sometimes wonder how they manage to fit them all on the touchline.

My counter-argument is that players like Cristiano Ronaldo or Thierry Henry wouldn't have lasted five minutes in my day... perhaps less! If I'd come up against a player like Ronaldo, within the first ten minutes I would have taken a good yellow card, something just short of red, to sort him out and then we'd see just how brave he really is. That's what makes me think that the likes of Messi and Ronaldo would have found it a lot harder if they'd been around then. Look back through the old clips and see the sort of treatment handed out to the flair players. See the kicks George

Best used to get and the way he just got up and got on with the game.

I'm not saying that players like Messi and Ronaldo shouldn't be protected, to a degree, because they are the sort of players who entertain the fans and we all want to see that. But football is a man's game after all and the more you do to wrap these players in cotton wool, the more you take out of the game as a real contest.

In the days before all the diving, feigning injury, whining to the referee and that type of thing, the flair players – and I'm thinking lads like Stan Bowles and Rodney Marsh – had to learn how to look after themselves. They knew how to ride a tackle and stay on their feet if they had a chance to score or create a goal. Nowadays, it seems like they would sooner go down and get an opponent booked than go on and get a shot in on goal. John Aldridge tells the one about when he was watching Man United one day and his wife came into the room with the hoover, vacuuming the floor; she nudged the TV and Ronaldo fell over! That just about sums them up.

I don't think there were many serial divers in my day. Of course we didn't have the TV analysis they have now so you can't be sure, but it was certainly not a regular feature of the game. The only one who you could say used to go down a bit too easily was Francis Lee. He had this crafty trick of tripping himself up with one foot behind the other when there was a defender on his shoulder. I think it was someone on *Match of the Day* who twigged onto the fact that he used to win more than his fair share of penalties.

It's very difficult for referees these days. Players are cute and know how to make it look like a foul when there has been little or no contact. But there is a sure-fire way to stop it, of course. The FA or the Premier League should put together a panel of four or five ex-pros and sit them down with videos of all the games: let's face it, anyone who has played the game at the highest level knows a dive when he sees one. Retrospective fines could then be imposed if someone is judged to have dived; two incidents and it's a one-game suspension, three strikes and they're out for several games. That would curb it.

The pity is that it seems to be the most gifted players who do it the most. They set a bad example and it's not what the viewing public want to see.

I played in an era when there was nothing like the fortunes washing about in football today, but I don't look at all those millionaire players like Suárez and wish it was me. Anyone who knows me will tell you it was never about the money. I never look at players today and think 'if only'. How could you put a price on the time I had playing in that great Liverpool team alongside Tommy Smith and my mate, Ray Kennedy? How could you value an FA Cup final with a struggling side like Brighton, or six years helping to keep Southampton among the elite? I would have done it just for the love.

The money that players receive today is obscene. I wouldn't think there is a player in the Premier League that isn't a millionaire and a great many of them are little better than average, so how the hell do you motivate someone like that?

I get a regular copy of the PFA magazine and it does make interesting reading, especially the adverts. Back in my day, they would be offering players the chance to buy a timeshare in Majorca; nowadays they advertise luxury apartments in Dubai. There are adverts for top-of-the-range kitchens, jewellery and watches... customise your Bentley! Now I don't want to sound like a grumpy old man but we had to pay for all our extras, we even took our own sandwiches on away trips. It helped us maintain a grip on reality. Nowadays, everything is done for the players, even down to getting their cars washed for them.

There are a lot of young players in the game today who don't even have to pull the shirt on and they are millionaires. I remember Mark Wright when he moved up to Liverpool. I played with him at Southampton in the mid-1980s and he was an exceptional defender. Then he moved to Derby and finally, in 1991, he got his big money transfer to Liverpool. He played well for them for a certain time but then I think he went off the boil for a bit. I was thinking about why and I reckon it was basically because he had become a millionaire overnight and it was at a time when Liverpool weren't pulling up any trees, so where was the incentive for him? He wasn't the worst by a long way. I think there some players who are happy just to pick their money up, even if they are stuck in the reserves. Whatever contract structures there are now, when I got into the first team I was on £300 a week, with a £150 a point bonus. That was the motivation to get into the team and stay there. Today, they get more than that just for wearing a particular brand of boots.

I've done OK out of football, looked after my money and earned myself a decent quality of life, but I don't think I've changed from the lad who used to play for the Blue and South Liverpool. I have never forgotten my place in the community. But there are a lot of players who think they are above everything; they have that 'don't you know who I am?' attitude and I think it's all down to money.

The one thing that football has brought me is a bit of recognition and sometimes it crops up in the most unusual circumstances. There was a time during the Southampton years when our manager Chris Nicholl decided to take the team on an end-of-season trip to Singapore for a four-team tournament. We were there for a week and naturally it included a bit of time off to see the sights, to have a little fun.

I was in a room with Kevin Bond and he used to like his gin and tonic so this one particular night we had a couple while we were getting suited and booted to go out for the evening. We came out of our hotel and decided to walk the mile or so along Orchard Road to meet the rest of the lads, who were waiting for us in a Kentucky Fried Chicken place. As we were walking along we noticed a Singapore police car alongside us, moving at our pace. I took a quick glance over and saw the police officer winding his window down. For a brief moment I wondered if we'd done something wrong, but he just said, 'You're Jimmy Case, aren't you?' and then he asked me to sign something for him.

Being a cheeky Scouser I asked if they could give Kevin and me a lift down to the KFC to meet the lads. 'Hop in,' he said and off we went. When we were about two blocks away from where the lads were waiting, I asked the policeman to put on the blue lights and we came to a sharp halt outside the

Kentucky. The lads couldn't believe what they were seeing when Kevin and me emerged from the back of the police car with a quick, 'Cheers, mate,' before they drove off.

Recognition can also open a few doors. It is not something I would ever ask for, but if opportunity arises, I'm not one to turn it down. And that's how I came to be backstage with Coldplay, at the Hollywood Bowl in Los Angeles. This story starts back in Liverpool, where a big mate of mine is Pete Byrne, who managed Echo and the Bunnymen, and also a guy named Ken Nelson, who was the producer of Coldplay. Pete took me to a Coldplay concert about fifteen years ago, back before they were a big international band, and from then on, I started watching them.

Coldplay's drummer, Will Champion, is a Southampton fan and I met him at St Mary's once after a game, took him into the Mick Channon lounge and we hit it off. So one night we went out for a drink to a local wine bar, but they wouldn't let Will in because he was wearing trainers. Fortunately, the owner knew me so I told Will to swap shoes with me and it would be OK. And that's how the drummer of Coldplay ended up wearing my shoes. It was the start of a good friendship.

I watched Coldplay's rise but our paths didn't cross again until I was on a trip to America in 2003. I had gone with Pete Byrne to see Echo and the Bunnymen in San Francisco. After the gig we headed down to Los Angeles, where Coldplay were due to give a concert in the LA Bowl, and through Pete we got backstage passes.

As Coldplay came off stage, Chris Martin's personal bodyguard, a man-mountain named Rocky, who just happened to be a

Liverpool fan, was waiting for him. Pete tapped Rocky on the shoulder and said, 'Can I introduce you to Jimmy Case?'

That was it. 'Follow me,' said Rocky, and with that he led us down the corridor and into the dressing room area for the after-show party. Then it was into a people carrier with Will and off to the Chateau Marmont hotel in Hollywood for a couple of beers. Tell you what, it was a bit of a step up from the Blue Union Stevedores and Dockers Social Club!

Another time, I had gone to see Iain McCulloch, lead singer from the Bunnymen, doing an acoustic set in London and I went back stage afterwards and Chris Martin was there. I just happened to be wearing this Coldplay T-shirt and it caught Chris's eye. On the back was a small Coldplay logo and on the front a handwritten set-list of songs that had been used at a concert. As we were chatting, Chris said, 'Where did you get that T-shirt?' I told him my daughter Jodie had got it off an Internet site and he looked at it and said, a bit angrily, 'I've not seen that one before.'

I said, 'What's the problem, mate?' and he replied, 'because it's my fucking handwriting!' He wasn't best pleased that someone had lifted it and made themselves a bob or two at his expense.

Meeting these people is not something that particularly interests me. As far as I am concerned, they are no different to you or me, but I can understand why people like to hang around the dressing rooms of these big stars. There is definitely a buzz in the air.

I've met a few, Cilla Black and Jimmy Tarbuck are both big Liverpool fans, and I remember Oliver Reed once coming to a

Brighton game and we got introduced. I knew about him from reading stuff in the papers about his antics. It was the only time I met him, but he seemed like a decent fella to me. He signed a programme for me; he wrote, 'To Jimmy, stitch that, Oliver Reed'!

I played in a charity golf match at Saunton Sands, and at the presentation in the evening, the organisers had got the Ryder Cup on show. It was too good a photo opportunity to pass up, especially when John Parrott, ex-snooker world champion, picked it up, so we all crowded round for the camera. John, of course, is a big Everton fan and as I walked past him, I couldn't resist the chance to have a little dig. 'It's not as heavy as the UEFA Cup,' I said, and then added, 'and the European Cup is even heavier.' He's a good lad is John and he took it in the right spirit... but I'm certain I could hear him swearing under his breath.

We had a good night, and nights like that are enjoyable, but to be perfectly honest, I am never happier than when I'm on the banks of the River Test with a fishing rod in my hand. Fishing is something I have done since I was a kid, starting off on Calderstones Park in Liverpool, just a short bike ride from my home. Then I started going a bit further afield, Ellesmere Lake. There was a gang of us, all about fourteen years old. I remember Graham Wren, Mark Kelly, Geoff Morris, Geoff Conalty and my brother Frank of course. We used to get the train out to the Wirral where there was this big viaduct over the canal. We would camp under one of the arches – sizzling bacon over an open fire for breakfast – and then fish all day. It's not something you can do now.

When I moved down to Southampton I was introduced to
a chap named Ralph Collins, who very sadly isn't with us
anymore after passing away a few years ago, who used to
manage the river. We arranged to meet just off the
Stocksbridge road and we hit it off straight away: he loved
football, I loved fishing.

He had three good stretches of river around the area of
Mottisfont Abbey between Romsey and Stockbridge. They
could only be fished by invitation and they were used by
politicians, entertainers like Eric Clapton... even the Queen of
Norway had been there. Ralph told me that one day he had
been on the river and on the opposite side was Eric
Morecambe. It's so peaceful, everyone in the world wants to
fish down there.

CHAPTER THIRTEEN

LIVERPOOL ARE BACK

There were times during the 2013/14 season, as Liverpool chased what had seemed back in August to be an impossible dream of a first championship for twenty-four years, when I sat quietly in the Anfield Press box and watched the Kop at their passionate best, the hairs on the back of my neck standing to attention.

With their colourful banners waving and swaying, strains of 'You'll Never Walk Alone' echoing around the grand old stadium, there were matches when the noise and atmosphere took me back to those great European nights of the seventies when the Kop made visitors tremble at the knees. As the years fell away, I could see Tommy Smith snapping into the tackle, remember Tosh at the far post heading down for Kevin Keegan to dive in where the boots were flying; I could even recall the odd missile from the right boot of one Jimmy Case.

The good times were back at last and Liverpool seemed to be on course for a remarkable triumph. Roared on by those fantastic, fanatical supporters, they were playing a brand of football that made even their harshest critics sit up and admire. The goals were flying in, top teams being brushed aside. From New Year's Day they set off on a run of results that brought fourteen wins, two draws and forty-nine goals from sixteen matches – now that's championship form in anyone's book.

Playing with freedom and spirit, they shared the supporters' dreams ... 'what if?', 'could they?' and 'they might'. But then, on 13 April 2014 everything changed. Suddenly, thanks to an unexpected gift from Vincent Kompany, in my view the Premier League's best defender, there was a shift in attitude when the outcome of the title race was placed firmly in Liverpool's hands. With three games to go, it was ours to win... but also ours to lose.

Three wins for the title, three wins for glory, three wins to end twenty-four years of hurt; twenty-four years of watching that lot from down the M62 equal and then pass Liverpool's record number of championship successes. As a player, and also as a fan, I know that, when thrust into that situation, suddenly the mindset changes. Liverpool couldn't face those final three games with the same cavalier attitude that had served them so well because now they knew they *had* to win those games to take the title, and that brings a different kind of pressure. The weight of expectation on the terraces, in the media, even in the dressing room, was cranked up and the truth is, Liverpool couldn't handle it. But I don't blame them one bit.

Because the one thing they didn't have to draw on in those final three, tense, nerve-shredding games, was experience. Only Glen Johnson as a title winner with Chelsea had a clear idea of what it was like to be on the threshold of such an incredible triumph. Faced with the chance to write a new chapter in the trophy-winning history of Liverpool FC, they simply weren't equipped to deal with it. I know it's easy from the Press box but I have no doubt in my mind that if Jamie Carragher could have been persuaded to play on for one more season Liverpool would have won the Premier League.

Why do I say that? Because Jamie knew how to organise a defence and that was the one crucial missing factor throughout the season, and particularly during those final decisive games. We had no problem scoring goals but there was always a nervousness about the defence because we lacked a leader at the back.

Against Chelsea, the momentary missed control by Steven Gerrard, followed by the slip as he tried to recover, would not have been so costly, had Carragher been there. Skrtel and Sakho had gone left and right, leaving Gerrard alone and exposed. Jamie would not have allowed that to happen. And against Crystal Palace, when we were coasting at 3–0, all that was needed was a calming voice at the back, someone who could organise the back four to keep things tight. Carragher would have done that. I wonder if he himself had similar thoughts as he watched from the stands.

When Liverpool were winning all those championships, back in the 1970s and 80s, there was always a nucleus of the side that had been there and done it. As new, younger players like myself were introduced into the team, there were always enough old heads around to prepare them for the demands of a title run-in. Brendan Rodgers' side didn't have that depth of experience to draw on.

The Liverpool of Shankly and Paisley played a similar pressure game with the same flair and pace. How else could they play with the likes of Stevie Heighway, Ian Callaghan, Terry McDermott, Emlyn Hughes and Ray Kennedy all on the pitch together? Those teams, including during my time at Anfield, were exciting to watch and scored goals for fun, but they also knew how to grind out a result when the situation demanded, and when, to use a modern phrase, to 'park the bus'.

Titles are decided over thirty-eight games and you end up where you deserve to be because of the number of points won over the entire season. But there is no getting away from the fact that the outcome of the 2013/14 season hinged on those final few games. The decisive result was the home defeat by Chelsea. That was the one that did the real damage and I have to say that on the day, Liverpool got it wrong, and it goes back to that change of mindset. The supporters felt it too. There was a certain degree of apprehension among the fans that day. I sensed it up in the Press box and it was clearly picked up by the players. They knew it was a game they really needed to win, perhaps they took it for granted they would win, but whatever was going through their minds, there is no doubt they pushed too hard against a tactically clever team organised by a tactically brilliant coach. Liverpool had all the possession but when the opening goal wouldn't come they lost patience and anxiety began to affect their decision-making. How else can you explain the situation which saw Steven Gerrard exposed as the last man, midway in his own half, when he made the fateful slip that let in Demba Ba?

They needed an option. The Liverpool side I played in favoured the passing game, just like Brendan's team, always keeping the ball on the deck. But Chelsea were set up to combat that and even though we got round the back of them, there was no aerial threat to exploit. Back in my day, I would get to the by-line and have at least three choices. I could drive it into the near post, where Kevin Keegan would be getting across the defender; I could pull it back to the edge of the box for Graeme Souness or Terry McDermott to have a shot; but if those openings were covered, I could just hang it up to the far post for John Toshack or Ray Kennedy to head home. I couldn't help thinking that with the likes of Joe Allen and Raheem Sterling, not the tallest of players, the team didn't really have that option. I remember saying on radio commentary that perhaps they could have sent on Daniel Agger to play up front and present the Chelsea back four with a different problem. In more recent years it was a fallback tactic we used to employ when Sami Hyypia was there, with a fair degree of success. Mind you, now he has signed Rickie Lambert to provide that aerial threat... I wonder if he was listening to me!

I was surprised by Mourinho's tactics, who usually sent out his Chelsea team to attack, certainly whenever they played Liverpool. Instead he went for a packed defence and a long ball up to Demba Ba. Was it out of respect for Liverpool that he came with such a negative attitude? I have another theory: Mourinho had been having a running battle with the FA as he wanted the game brought forward to the Saturday to give him more time to prepare for the important Champions League clash with Atletico Madrid. True to form, the FA wouldn't budge, so I reckon Mourinho threw his toys out of the pram and said, 'Sod you, I'm not playing – and I don't care if it is on TV', and they proceeded to bore everyone into submission. The fact that they won the game was more by luck than judgment. Without Gerrard's unfortunate slip, it would have been a different story.

A few days later, Liverpool went three goals up at Crystal Palace, playing their usual sharp, penetrative football against an in-form side. Tony Pulis had done a fantastic job at Selhurst Park and, backed by some of the noisiest fans in the League, it was a real challenge, so to dominate them as Liverpool did was a terrific effort. It put them right back in the title race and at that point, like the Liverpool of old, they should have killed the game by maintaining their defensive shape and retaining possession of the football. Especially when Palace pulled one back, which was the warning sign to shut up shop. But they didn't have the collective knowledge to make that happen and in the heat of the moment, panicked. Had Carragher been there to marshal the defence, I'm sure we would have won that game to put a bit of pressure on Manchester City. But because of that collapse, by the time the final games came around, the dream had gone. It needed an improbable trail of events, like Andy Carroll scoring for West Ham from a Stewart Downing cross. Imagine that happening! But no one really expected City to slip up because they have a squad full of players who know how to handle the pressure at its most intense and you cannot put a price on that level of experience.

There was a deep sense of disappointment hanging over Anfield as the announcement was made that City were champions. You could see it in the players' eyes, none more than Steven Gerrard, a Scouser like me and the player who is the heart and soul of the side. I certainly felt it. As an ex-player and a fully paid-up member of the Liverpool fan club I was gutted. But in the same breath I was immensely proud of the way Liverpool had gone about their work for most of the season and I share the gratitude all the fans feel for the way Brendan Rodgers and his team have restored that pride for the club and the city.

Yes, they fell short at the final hurdle, but when you think about where the team has come from in such a short space of time, and the progress players like Jordan Henderson, Raheem Sterling, Joe Allen, John Flanagan and yes, even Luis Suárez, have made under the astute guidance of Rodgers, the over-riding emotion has to be one of optimism because this Liverpool team can only learn from the experience and will undoubtedly be all the stronger for it.

I wouldn't suggest for a minute that Brendan Rodgers should change Liverpool's style. The team bristles with pacy and aggressive players and is geared up to play progressive, attacking football. That is the manager's philosophy and it clearly works. When the disappointment has faded away, as it surely will, they can look back with a great deal of satisfaction at what they have achieved. Second place in the toughest league in the world is a measure of the remarkable progress they have made in the two seasons since Rodgers took over. They are now above Chelsea, Arsenal, Tottenham and, it warms my heart to say it, Manchester United. With Rodgers at the helm, there is no reason why they cannot stay there and aim even higher because they will be all the better for knowing what more is needed to hang on the next time they reach the summit.

Singling out Rodgers for praise is in no way intended to play down the contribution of every player that pulled on the shirt during the past season. They have been exceptional – but Liverpool have had exceptional players in the past who have not been able to deliver a championship: players like Robbie Fowler, Michael Owen, Jamie Carragher, Stan Collymore, Paul Ince, Jamie Redknapp, Dietmar Hamann, Jason McAteer... it's a long list. But unlike some of the managers since 1990, a list that includes Ronnie Moran, Graeme Souness, Roy Evans, Gérard Houllier, Rafa Benitez, Roy Hodgson, even King Kenny, Brendan Rodgers has somehow found a formula that works. He has created the formation, inspired and coached the players and, most importantly, reignited the passion of the fans.

I didn't think he could do it, certainly not within twenty-one months of taking the job. He came with good credentials as a young coach who believed in possession football with the emphasis on attack. The way he set up his Swansea team had to be admired, but I didn't look at him and immediately think yes, this is the man to resurrect Liverpool FC. But since arriving at Anfield he has gone about his work in a quiet, calm, measured style and you only have to look closely into his eyes to realise that he also has the steely resolve all successful managers must possess.

He came into a difficult situation. Luis Suárez had been banned for ten games after the biting incident with the Chelsea defender Branislav Ivanovic. All the signs were there that Suárez would never play for Liverpool again. But Rodgers came up with a different script and he got it spot on. He persuaded Suárez that the future at Liverpool was going to be better under his guidance, and at the same time he reminded the player of his responsibilities to the club and to the fans. He managed to convince Suárez that he would find no better platform anywhere in the world for his talents and in so doing provided the team with the goal machine it needed to fire a title-chasing campaign. And then, just for good measure, he gave him a £12m striking partner in Daniel Sturridge.

When Suárez arrived at Liverpool from Ajax, he came with a reputation as an aggressive player and I liked the sound of that. But he has to learn that you can have that aggression without going around biting people. It is certainly not the right thing to do, especially in this day and age when the TV cameras pick up everything that happens from every angle. But we all do things we are not supposed to do; like the time I had three of Regi Blinker's dreadlocks in my hand... you are not supposed to do that either, but to this day I don't know how they got there. Maybe it is something to do with where Suárez comes from. When they have fights in Uruguay, perhaps they bite you. I don't suppose they fight by the Queensberry rules.

He was given a ten-game ban for the Ivanovic offence, but I reckon the FA got that wrong. Liverpool should have appealed against the length of the ban. They should have asked the FA to reduce the number of games for which he was suspended... if he agreed to wear a muzzle for the rest of the season!

He was on the wrong end of a media witch-hunt and probably a bit disillusioned with life at the club. It can happen when the team isn't good enough for you. Liverpool had gone through a big upheaval and looked like they had lost their way. They weren't able to sign the type of players needed to take them to the top level because they weren't in the Champions League. For a player of Suárez's calibre, if the team cannot give him the service he needs, he can soon become frustrated. Over the years Liverpool have always had top strikers: from my day when we had Kevin and Kenny, then Ian Rush, John Aldridge, Robbie Fowler, Michael Owen; some of the best goal-scorers in the game. But if they hadn't had the right back-up, players who could get the ball into the right place at the right time and with the right pace, they wouldn't have scored that many goals. So I think he might have been a bit disillusioned at the time because it didn't look as if Liverpool were capable of reaching the same level he was striving for.

I can identify with Suárez as a player. His only motivation

when he steps over the white line is to win... whatever it takes. You can see it in his work ethic, his bravery, his aggression, his sheer determination. That's what makes a winner, something the England team could do with more of. You can see it in the way he slaughters his own players if they don't make the right pass; you can see it in the way he beats himself up if he misses a chance; you can see it in the pleasure he gets from scoring goals.

He reminds me of Ian Rush, the way he puts defenders, even the goalkeeper, under pressure. Like a dog with a bone, he keeps going back for it and never gives them a moment's peace. But he also reminds of me of Kenny Dalglish because of his ability on the ball, how he can make a pass with either foot, his quickness of thought and vision, coupled with the ability to execute what he sees. And he is also a swashbuckling type of player, just like Kevin Keegan was. When he gets the ball his first thought is to score a goal and I like that selfishness.

That was evident when he first arrived, but as I said the team wasn't good enough for him at that point; it wasn't set up in a way that would bring the best out of him. He still played well. Let's face it, the man either plays brilliantly or great. There are no bad games with Suárez. But it is understandable that players like him can get disillusioned if the team and the tactics do not complement his ability and that's where frustration can lead to a negative reaction.

We all know the kind of stuff that goes on all the time in a game. Players have always tried to wind each other up. Dennis Wise used to pinch me under the armpit and, let me tell you, that hurts. When the adrenalin is flowing it takes you to the edge. But there is a line that should never be crossed and biting an opponent certainly crosses the line. Suárez plays it down as something that just happens, but I have never heard of players biting each other before. Simply, it is unacceptable.

So, like everyone else, I thought Rodgers had helped him conquer that dark side of his character and, certainly, his performances for Liverpool during the chase for the title suggested he had got his head straight. That was why it was such a shock to see Suárez do what he did in Brazil, putting the bite on the Italian defender Giorgio Chiellini.

No-one will be more disappointed by what happened than Brendan Rodgers. Watching Suárez lead Liverpool to the brink of the title, he must have thought he had slayed the dragon.

Now Suárez has reached a crossroads in his career. The latest ban, four months and barred from entering any stadium, shows that Fifa will not tolerate that sort of behaviour. He may be one of the most highly-valued, best-paid players in the world, but if he wants to be acknowledged among the modern greats like Messi and Ronaldo, he has to change. He has to learn – with the help of family, friends, colleagues, counsellors or whatever it takes – to control the demon, otherwise he will be hounded out of the game. And that would be a sad day indeed.

Luis Suarez wasn't the only problem Rodgers had to tackle. There was another puzzle to solve, by the name of Raheem Sterling. Here was a young player with serious ability, blistering pace and a decent football brain. He had the world at his feet: fame, talent, loaded with cash while still a teenager, but there were signs that he could be about to throw it all away. He was making headlines for the wrong reasons; someone had to take him to one side and make him grow up. I don't know how Rodgers did it. Carrot and stick, an arm round his shoulder and then a bollocking, or perhaps he just reminded him that he was a Liverpool player and with that shirt comes a responsibility. If you fail to live up to the Anfield standards then you have no future there... and I speak from experience.

I like the way Rodgers speaks: he doesn't get carried away, never looks further than the next game, but unlike some, he never plays down what Liverpool can and should achieve. At the start of the season no one saw Liverpool as title challengers, but at no point did Rodgers say they couldn't do it. He didn't thump his chest and predict Liverpool would be champions, but he never once wrote off their chances.

When we had thumped Spurs 4–0 on a day when Anfield was rocking with more than forty-four thousand fans packed into the ground, Rodgers said after the game, 'The dream is for our supporters, they want to win the title – but it is not in my thinking. My thinking is to prepare the team and perform well and if we do that, we can continue to win games and then we can see where that takes us.'

At first it was for the fans. It was vital for Rodgers, as the new manager, that they bought into the idea that nothing was impossible. He needed them with him, not against him. But as the season wore on, and particularly as Liverpool went on that amazing run of wins that took them to the top, he refused to rule it out.

That sort of talk is music to a player's ears. It was how Shanks and Bob Paisley used to talk. Bill Shankly would convince players they could produce things they probably thought were beyond them. When he gave us a pre-match talk, I used to go out on the pitch feeling ten feet tall. Bob, on the other hand, was the master at bringing us back down to earth.

When I go back to Anfield these days, I can hear Shanks' voice echoing down the corridor, 'Aye, son, ye'll do for me!' I can hear Bob Paisley's familiar northeast accent saying, 'Alright lad – same again.' Rodgers has brought back Shankly's spirit and Bob's sense of peace. But above all that, for me he has given Liverpool FC back to the people. He has gone out of his way to make everyone at the club feel part of his revolution, just with a quiet word and a friendly gesture. He talks to everyone: staff, volunteers, old players, visitors... and especially the fans.

Brendan Rodgers makes no secret of the fact that he wants to re-establish the Liverpool dynasty created by Shanks and maintained by Bob Paisley. For too long the club has played in the shadow of United and he is determined to reverse that situation. I reckon the signs are good. Not only are Liverpool going to get better, but United are a team in transition, their star players getting old, the club attempting to recover from a position of weakness and decline.

City are clearly the team to beat now. Champions again,

they can throw any amount of money at staying on top. What they lack is a real connection between the team and its fans. Not one homegrown player in their side. Not one player who has come through the youth system and can honestly say he is Manchester City through and through. Liverpool have Gerrard, Flanagan, Sterling and more in the pipeline who know that if they are good enough, they will be given their chance by Rodgers.

As for the London lot... Arsenal haven't the gumption to invest the kind of sums needed to establish a team capable of dominating the domestic game; Spurs are the same inconsistent bunch they have always been. Chelsea are the best of the Southerners. It was Mourinho's first season back and despite not having a striker worthy of the name, he steered them into title contention and deep into the Champions League. If he is true to his word and stays at Stamford Bridge for a few years, his coaching ability, backed by the Russian's money, could establish Chelsea as the dominant force of the next decade. It will be fascinating to watch them, City and Liverpool fighting it out.

What none of Liverpool's rivals have got is a twelfth man like the Anfield support. I'm not sure if opposition players these days are quite so intimidated, certainly not players at the top clubs: they are all internationals, they have all played in big games, in big stadiums, in front of big crowds. No, it is what the Kop does for the Liverpool players that makes all the difference. They provide the inspiration to find an extra yard of pace, an extra ounce of power in the tackle, another lungful of breath to get up and back.

I don't think some of our previous managers have truly understood that. Certainly not the foreign coaches like Houllier and Benitez; not even an English coach like Roy Hodgson. He might have understood it, but he wasn't a Liverpool sort of manager; he didn't know how to make the connection. It took Bill Shankly a good few years to build that unique relationship. Paisley had been alongside him as he did it so he understood, but it is difficult for an outsider to feel the passion and use it the way they did.

When Rodgers took on the job of rejuvenating Liverpool he realised he had to get the fans on his side. 'It is a monumental size of club and when we have that support behind us it is a real force,' he said. How true is that? I played in games where the supporters made us feel invincible. When we felt the love and passion that was pouring down on us from the terraces, there was no way we would yield, because no one wanted to let those supporters down.

Now it is Brendan Rodgers' turn to harness the power of the Kop and use it to give them a team that will become as dominant as my Liverpool. It is a big task that reads: Clemence, Neal, Smith, Thompson, Kennedy, Hughes, Dalglish, Case, Heighway, Souness, McDermott.

So, can he do it? Can he emulate the achievements of Shanks and Bob Paisley? His team will be energised by the past season's experience, hurt by the disappointment, determined to go one better; and although the final step is the most difficult, I firmly believe the title is now within Liverpool's reach. I can honestly see the championship trophy being displayed at Anfield in the not-too-distant future and I promise you this: I will be there, watching and hoping with the rest of the Anfield faithful.

Once a Scouser...

CHAPTER FOURTEEN

WHAT THE OTHERS SAY

CO-AUTHOR ANDREW SMART GAUGES POPULAR OPINION ABOUT JIMMY CASE.

I wasn't expecting the Jimmy Case I met in the London office of publisher John Blake. I remember him as a player, mainly from a few crunching appearances against Nottingham Forest, the team I supported, and who proved to be Liverpool's great rivals, back in the late 1970s; and for that remarkable FA Cup final goal against Manchester United, which starts this memoir.

He had a reputation then as a hard man, a player who didn't take prisoners, a footballer who left his mark on many a star performer. By definition, he should have been a tough guy to talk to, perhaps a little defensive about his popular image, guarded about some of the more painful, even embarrassing, incidents in which he had been involved, on and off the field. But he wasn't like that at all. Quiet, unassuming, modest and totally open, he was something of a revelation. Charming and relaxed, funny and sincere, I liked him from the moment we met and we got on like a house on fire.

It made the job of writing this book so much easier. Jimmy's recall from his very earliest days growing up in Liverpool and on to one of the most illustrious careers any professional footballer could wish for brought back a host of memories: funny, sad, daft and serious, all of them intrinsically fascinating. He has just passed his sixtieth birthday yet he looks twenty years younger, still lean and fit without an ounce of excess fat on the parts most old footballers last saw in their youth. In fact, he looks about the same as he did when he played his last professional game at the age of forty-one.

Jimmy Case is a true Scouser, but his accent has softened over the many years he has spent living on the south coast. 'It gets stronger every time I go back home and meet up with old mates, over a pint or two,' he remarked during one of our long chats. And that sums up the essence of Case, a legendary footballer but also a good man who has never forgotten his roots.

We talked about the players he admired, team-mates and opponents, and I trawled through hours of TV action footage and interviews to get the inside story on Jimmy Case. One thing emerged, one consistent feature from his days at Liverpool and on to Brighton, to Southampton, and wherever else he plied his trade. It is hard to find anyone with a bad word to say about him, apart from Evertonians, of course.

Kevin Keegan was the star performer at Anfield when Jimmy made his debut, back in 1975. 'I remember him joining us at Liverpool from South Liverpool, a non-league club,' recalled the former England captain and manager. 'His fee then was something like £500, which was laughable when you think of the price of all the players around us then and the value they were.

'He came in with a tremendous attitude and looked very much at home with players who, really, if you judged by price, should have been much better than him.

'But he had a great attitude and worked very hard, he was a real team player and a very willing lad... he had no ego and that was what I liked about him.

'He achieved an awful lot. He's got a lot of medals in his cupboard and he deserved every one of them. He has always been a smashing lad and good to have around your club and obviously good to have with you on the football field.

'One way of putting it is that he is just the person you would want with you in the trenches in a war... you'd look to your right and see Jimmy Case.

'My last league game was against Brighton for Newcastle and Jimmy Case was in the Brighton team and he was the first to come over to me at the end to say it was a shame I was packing it in. I thought it was nice that, when I was finishing, someone who actually meant something to me was actually involved in the same game.

'If anyone said to me, do I remember a good game of Jimmy's I could think of loads, but if you said to me, think of a bad game, I can't think of any.'

In his own inimitable Geordie way, Lawrie McMenemy, the manager of Southampton FC who signed Jimmy for a paltry £30,000 in 1985, put his finger on the soul of this quiet man of football. Speaking back in 1994, McMenemy said, 'To say that Jimmy Case has not had a brilliant career would be as ludicrous as saying that someone would waste time at a corner kick when his team is three up with only three minutes to go!

'The fact is that Jimmy's career flourished at the highest level with Liverpool, where he never got the credit he deserved simply because he was the local lad playing amongst a host of very expensive and very talented imported "stars" from other clubs, but like most local lads, he had to leave home to get more appreciation.

'I know for a fact that if you mentioned his name now on Merseyside every one of those supporters will class Jimmy as being one of their best ever players.

'When I brought him to The Dell from Brighton for £30,000, I must say that I thought he would fill in until the end of the season, when I would be able to bring in a younger and better midfield player.

'Jimmy, however, outlasted me and carried on to play two hundred and fifteen games for the club and endeared himself for all time to the lovers of good players who regularly attend The Dell.

'His style of football is simple and effective. He is the perfect link man and is always able to assist both defenders and attackers when they are in trouble. He has always been quite happy for others to take the plaudits, but professionals know how effective and how good he has been during a long and glittering career.

'I well remember the day he sat in my office to talk about

signing. He was smart and trendy, with his long hairstyle. I thought it was a little strange that he sat sideways on to me, especially when I talked to him about the terms of his contract. It was not until weeks later when I tried to talk to him about tactics in the dressing room and he turned the other side to me that I realised how deaf he was and the long hair covered one of the biggest hearing aids I have ever seen.

'He did not need me or, I suspect, anyone else during his career to tell him how to play football. He was quite simply a natural, a real star and more important, an extremely nice man.'

Among the up-and-coming young players in that Southampton team of the late 1980s was a no-nonsense defender by the name of Neil Ruddock, who was building a double reputation: a decent player but also a bit of a loose cannon likely to get sent off with every tackle he made.

Ruddock would go on to play more than a hundred times for Liverpool, win an England cap and make more than three hundred and fifty appearances in a career lasting nearly twenty years, but as he was learning his trade he needed someone to get hold of him and turn his life around. Jimmy Case was the man for the job.

'Jimmy was Saints captain at the time and he took me under his wing and gave me a good rollocking and put me on the right road. He took me on one side and said that I could go two ways, "You either keep getting booked and make a name for yourself or calm down a bit and get on in the game".

'At the time at Southampton there was Rodney Wallace,

Alan Shearer, Matt Le Tissier, Tim Flowers and me all together and he brought us through.

'He was our captain at the time and he made us conduct ourselves in the right manner.

'I learned my trade playing with him. After most games he would take me to one side and give me hints as to what he thought I should be doing.

'Despite getting on so well with him I never thought I would follow him to Liverpool. I'd moved back to Tottenham, which I thought was a dream move for me... there are not many bigger clubs than Tottenham but Liverpool is one of them.

'I had a few teams after me – Newcastle, Chelsea, Forest and Blackburn as well as Liverpool all wanted to sign me – so I rang Jimmy up to ask what he thought and he told me that, without a shadow of a doubt, I should sign for Liverpool. 'It's the best city in the world to play football when you are winning... if you lose, it's not the best place to play.'

Another of those youngsters went on to play sixty-three times for England and became the highest scorer in Premier League history. Instantly recognisable today as a top TV pundit, his name is Alan Shearer.

'I certainly learned from Jimmy how to look after myself. He was great, his all-round game and his personality were tremendous. If you couldn't learn from him then you shouldn't really be in the game.

'It was a big disappointment for me when he left Southampton because there was a lot of talk about him becoming manager at The Dell, but Ian Branfoot came in and released him. I don't think I was the only one who was disappointed. His departure was a big loss to his team-mates and the supporters alike.

'I remember one game... against Manchester United in the Cup. Although he didn't score, he played a big part in our win. We had a lot of youngsters in the team at that time and he had done and seen it all before, his talking helped us through.

'It is quite remarkable that he never got a cap. He must be one of the unluckiest men in the game not to have been honoured.

'I will always remember how much Jimmy did for me. He was there when I needed him, he put me on the right tracks at Southampton.'

Shearer highlighted the one glitch in Jimmy's career, the glaring omission in his list of achievements: the fact that he never won a full England cap. He has talked within these pages about his disappointment, about being the odd man out among Liverpool's legion of internationals, and to this day, he still cannot fully understand why the call-up never came, especially at a time when he was a key member of that all-conquering Liverpool team of the late 1970s.

That same question was posed by the great Liam Brady, Irish international and Arsenal hero, who was Jimmy's manager on his second coming at Brighton, at a time when the future of the club was teetering on the brink of collapse.

Liam said, 'It is difficult to know where to start when talking about Jimmy Case. But if I start with him as a player it would be to describe a very, very fine midfield player who was grossly under-rated in his prime and it is quite amazing to me that he was never capped for England in his Liverpool days.

'He was probably still worth a cap when he played for Brighton and Southampton but it might not have helped his England chances then, being with an unfashionable club.

'He was always a very tough opponent and very difficult to play against and he is a person you want on your side rather than against you. Things were pretty bad when we took over and Jimmy was my first signing. Immediately he had a real presence on the field and he was exactly what was needed at that particular time.'

And while we're in the company of stellar footballers, here is what Kenny Dalglish – the man Jimmy reckons is the best he ever played with – had to say about him.

'I first met Jimmy Case in August 1977 when I signed for Liverpool. The first game I had for the club was in the Charity Shield and in those days we used to travel to London by train.

'Coming back, Jimmy was one of four lads with whom I shared a compartment. He immediately struck me as being a very deep person. He was always good company and, while he was quite a private person, it was on the pitch that he could really express himself.

'He did a magnificent job playing where he did for Liverpool. He played wide right and he always had a lot more to offer than he was perhaps allowed to. It wasn't really until he moved away from Liverpool that his value was really appreciated by those still there. He had an awful lot of skill but much of it was sacrificed for the needs of the team.

'He was desperately unlucky not to be capped by England.

It would have been great if he had got an international cap, even if just for his contribution, which did so much for others during games.

'It is always sad to see people go and when he left Liverpool it was a sad day. He went to Brighton and came back to haunt us. I played in the Fifth Round FA Cup game in 1983 when he scored a deflected goal just as we got back in the game.

'I have my own ideas on why he was so good at Liverpool. He's deaf in one ear and I reckon he always used to turn the deaf ear towards the dugout. I could shout in his left ear because I knew how to make him hear, so we got on all right.'

There are many more tributes to Jimmy Case to draw on, comments from contemporaries who believe he was arguably the best player never to be capped for his country; others from opponents who agree he was the hardest they ever faced, but it is also worthwhile taking a view from the other side, from the Press benches, where critics sit and pass largely uneducated verdicts on performance and character. The relationship between players and the Press is not always comfortable; footballers are known to be a tad prickly when criticised. It was never a problem for Jimmy.

The late John Vinicombe was another legend in football. As chief sports writer for the *Brighton Evening Argus*, he was a highly respected journalist who had an eloquent way with words. When Jimmy Case was awarded a richly deserved testimonial game at the old Goldstone Ground in 1994, against Liverpool, of course, Vinicombe contributed his own tribute to the souvenir programme, which he began with a statement of fact, 'If ever an Albion player was secure in the Goldstone Hall of Fame, it is Jimmy Case.

'As favourites go, they don't rate any higher than Jimmy. Not once have I heard a Brighton voice raised against him. And, so far as the North Standers are concerned, Case walks on water and is, without doubt, the Main Man.

'The reason is not difficult to fathom. The real fans realised what a totally committed pro Jimmy was as soon as he stepped on to the pitch. Perhaps they didn't need any convincing for Case's talents were already well documented with his native Liverpool.

'But suddenly there he was in Seagull gear after another much-admired player, Mark Lawrenson, had travelled in the opposite direction.

'I remember as if it was yesterday the deal going through at a hotel near Heathrow in August 1981. Albion chairman Mike Bamber wrapped up a record deal for both clubs when Lawrenson was sold for a million and Case, valued at £350,000, agreed to become a Seagull.

'Mike Bamber and John Smith, the Liverpool chairman, shook hands while Jimmy was doing press-ups in the corridor.

'Very soon Case commanded a following that almost reached the proportions of adulation that had been bestowed on Peter Ward... Jimmy's dynamic shooting and uncompromising attitude when going for a 50–50 ball had the crowd eating out of his hand.

'It was Jimmy's good fortune that he played in the same [Liverpool] team as [Tommy] Smith... this explains why Case's appetite for the fray has remained undiminished over twenty years. The distinction of being England's oldest full-time outfielder is a mantle that still sits lightly on his broad shoulders.

'In classic fashion, the head manifestly saves the legs, but the bear-trap tackle is still there even if Jimmy has dropped the finger wagging ritual that always let an opponent know that an act of retribution would be exacted as surely as night followed day.

'Big Lawrie [McMenemy] was not wrong in returning Jimmy to the elite and, as I understand it, the preliminary discussions spoke volumes for the new signing.

'When he asked McMenemy if he could stay living in Hove, the boss came back with, "I'm told you like a drink."

'Jimmy's reply was typically candid, "That's right, I do." McMenemy knew he was dealing with a man, not a jack-the-lad or callow youth. "I don't need to keep an eye on you, I trust you," was the reply and Jimmy was a Saint.

'Like any good pro, he loves a party, but has the good sense to know when to stop. When Albion needed a laugh to break the tension on the road to Wembley, it usually came from Case. "We had a lot of laughs. Apart from my hearing aid, we had Gordon Smith, Neil Smillie and Eric Young all with contact lenses. Someone said if they had a bell in the ball and then painted it luminous orange, Manchester United wouldn't have stood a chance. After that all we needed was a one-legged centre forward – though Michael Robinson did his best to fill that role."

'Curiously, Jimmy can often hear perfectly well when there is a lot of background noise. He has slept through fire alarms and given some funny answers to simple questions. Tony Grealish once asked him how many times he had played at Wembley. Case didn't quite get it all, looked at his watch and said, "Oh, about 3.30.'"

Never one to get carried away by praise or achievement, Jimmy said in response, 'I know I have a good relationship with ex-players because that's the way I am. I cannot say I dislike any one of them. We might have had differences, but they were soon forgotten.

'To get stuff off the likes of Lawrie, Kevin and Kenny... well, it means a lot because of the people they are and because of what I achieved with them.'

So, is there anything left to be said about Jimmy Case? Well, of course the final words must come from his best friend Ray Kennedy, one of the shining stars of football in the 1970s but whose life has been blighted by the pernicious grip of Parkinson's Disease. His playing days were well in the past when Jimmy was given his testimonial match in 1994, but despite his pain and discomfort, Ray made the long trip from his home in the northeast to honour his pal. Naturally, it was Jimmy who picked him up from the airport.

Ray said, 'I first met Jimmy Case at Liverpool when I came to Anfield from Arsenal and we both played many times together.

'He had come into League football late but when he made the League side we started to share a room together on all the club trips and soon became firm friends.

'We have had great times together but simply being in his company means a lot to me... we got to know each other so well. We must have made hundreds of cups of tea for each other over the years.

'Many people don't give credit to Jimmy as a personality in his own right. He had a reputation for being one of the workhorses at Liverpool but he was much more than that and he has proved himself by going on to the age of forty and still doing well.

'It is not just his body strength and fitness that has allowed him to do that, he wants to play and it is just another example of how he does not let anybody down.

'He is so reliable... it's brilliant!

'I frequently have to go to hospital in London these days and Jimmy always makes it up to see me. It doesn't seem to matter to him if he's been at Darlington or Wrexham, he's still made it to London to see me.

'We spent eight years together. He very quickly became my best friend in football and my best friend out of football. He never let me down and I am sure never will.'